George Peck

Our Country

Its Trial and Its Triumph

George Peck

Our Country

Its Trial and Its Triumph

ISBN/EAN: 9783337227012

Printed in Europe, USA, Canada, Australia, Japan

Cover: Foto ©Andreas Hilbeck / pixelio.de

More available books at **www.hansebooks.com**

OUR COUNTRY:

ITS TRIAL AND ITS TRIUMPH.

A Series of Discourses

SUGGESTED BY THE VARYING EVENTS OF THE WAR
FOR THE UNION.

By GEORGE PECK, D.D.

———◆●◆———

New York:
PUBLISHED BY CARLTON & PORTER,
200 MULBERRY-STREET.
1865.

Entered according to Act of Congress, in the year 1865, by

CARLTON & PORTER,

in the Clerk's Office of the District Court of the United States for the Southern District of New York.

PREFACE.

THE discourses which compose this volume were suggested by the events of the day, and were delivered while those events were still current in the thoughts and the hearts of the people. They are arranged here chiefly in accordance with the order of time. The sermon on "Our Heritage" occupies the first position, because it forms a fitting introduction to the general subject. The second, on "Obedience to the Civil Authority," was preached in the summer of 1861, when the nation began to realize that a war of gigantic proportions was upon us, and Christian men were earnestly inquiring the path of duty. The third, on "The Signs of the Times," was preached at a camp-meeting in the valley of Wyoming, about the time of the second battle of Bull Run. The fifth is a sermon delivered in Scranton, Pa., on the day of National Thanksgiving after the victory at Gettysburgh. Thus, one by one, as the varying events of the war suggested, the discourses were prepared and delivered, and a number of them were published in the local newspapers. They have been carefully revised, and are now offered to the public with the hope that their publication may not be wholly in vain in this the day of our national trial.   G. P.

SCRANTON, PA., *March* 4, 1865.

CONTENTS.

		PAGE
I.	OUR HERITAGE	7
II.	OBEDIENCE TO CIVIL GOVERNMENT	20
III.	THE SIGNS OF THE TIMES	36
IV.	STRENGTH IN THE DAY OF ADVERSITY	57
V.	FIERY TRIALS OF OUR FREE INSTITUTIONS	69
VI.	RADICALISM	90
VII.	THE LORD'S CONTROVERSY	104
VIII.	THE WRATH OF MAN SHALL PRAISE GOD	122
IX.	SLAVERY	139
X.	A COMPROMISE REJECTED	169
XI.	NO NEUTRALITY	187
XII.	NO FALSE PEACE	203
XIII.	HARDER BLOWS, AND MORE OF THEM	217
XIV.	THE SECESSION DEVIL	231
XV.	THE GOOD SAMARITAN	256

OUR COUNTRY:
ITS TRIAL AND ITS TRIUMPH.

I.

OUR HERITAGE.

THE LINES ARE FALLEN UNTO ME IN PLEASANT PLACES; YEA, I HAVE
A GOODLY HERITAGE.—Psa. xvi, 6.

In this world, though crowded with moral and physical evils, there are "pleasant places." In the midst of wars and rumors of wars there are intervals of peace. While the ear is stunned with bacchanalian revels and noisy mirth, there may be found the temple of worship and the quiet family altar.

When surrounded by jagged rocks, yawning chasms, and stagnant pools, myriads of beautiful landscapes, variegated by the greensward, the yellow grain, and the waving corn, greet the eye. Beautiful flowers regale the sight and delicious fruits invite the taste. Among the monarchies and despotisms which wage war against human progress and crush out the freedom of the soul, there is one free republic where liberty has full scope. While large portions of the world are surrounded by the moral blight of heathenism and popery, there is a true Church of God crowned with salvation and reflecting the glory of the Redeemer. The prospect is not all dark and forbidding, but the eye is cheered with physical beauty, while the heart is charmed with moral splendors. The people whose local habitation is surrounded with pleasurable objects are happy.

If there is a country on the map of the world truly favored of God it is our own America. We have a country, a government, and a Church bequeathed to us, primarily by God, and secondarily by our fathers, which constitute a rich heritage, and which demand of us in return patriotism and religion.

We have a goodly heritage.

This country has "lines," or definite boundaries. The text refers to the lot which fell to the Israelites in Canaan. Their land originally included the country from the Arabian desert on the south to the mountains of Lebanon on the north, and from the river Jordan on the east to the Mediterranean sea on the west. Under the reign of David it embraced all the territory between the Euphrates and the Mediterranean, or "from the river to the ends of the earth," or the land's end. (See 1 Kings iv, 21, 22, and Psa. lxxii, 8.) The larger territory was all embraced in the promise given to Abram. (Gen. xiii, 15.)

There is a striking analogy between the lines of the land of Israel and those of our own country. Originally the land divided by Joshua embraced little more than a narrow strip of country between the Jordan and the Mediterranean; but ultimately, under Solomon, it covered the whole country between the Euphrates and the border of Egypt. (1 Kings iv, 21.) Originally we only had thirteen states, embracing the country from the Atlantic to Lake Erie, and from the Canada line to the southern boundary of Georgia. Ultimately we became possessed of the whole territory between the Atlantic and the Pacific, and from the British possessions on the north to the Gulf of Mexico on the south. These are our lines to-day. This vast territory has come into our possession, so far as human agency is concerned, partly by conquest, and partly by purchase from other nations and the Indian tribes. The providence of God being concerned in the whole arrangement, we should regard our country as a divine gift, an inheritance conferred by Him who rules over the affairs of nations, "setting up one and putting down another."

The lines are fallen to us in pleasant places. This is truly "a delightsome land" in the beauty of its natural scenery; its towering mountains, with their fertile slopes; its vast rivers, with their luxuriant vales clothed with every variety of flowers and fruitage, loaded with agricultural wealth, and crowded with animal life of every variety. We have the gay bloom and golden fruit of the tropics, and the glistening glaciers of the Rocky Mountain heights; the rapid but short-lived vegetation of Lake Champlain, and the perennial verdure of the gulf states. Whatever of beauty invites the eye upon the plains of Italy or on Alpine heights, is found here in profusion.

The splendid moving palaces which crowd our seaboard, and thread in all their windings the Connecticut, the Hudson, the Ohio, the Mississippi, and the Missouri, add a new element of beauty to the rockbound ocean, and the streams which rush from the mountains, meander through the vales, and form bays in connection with the great ocean. The rapidity of transit unites all extremes, bringing together autumn and spring, winter and summer, and heightening the interest by the contrast.

Hitherto I have dwelt mostly upon the sources of pleasure opened in the beautiful and interesting scenes presented to view in such abundance in this goodly land. Let us next survey the resources of this country as it regards material wealth and physical comfort.

We have a soil of unsurpassed productiveness, furnishing every variety of grains, grasses, roots, and fruits in luxurious abundance. The hand of industry is everywhere rewarded with the most ample yield of food for man and beast. Our commerce pours in a ceaseless tide of wealth, our merchant ships visiting every part of the world, and our sails whitening every sea. Our mineral wealth seems without bounds. The gold of California, and of the slopes of the Rocky Mountains; the lead and copper of the western states, and the coal and ores of Pennsylvania, are sources of boundless wealth to the nation. Our manufactories produce an abundance of the means of domestic comfort and a state of advanced civilization. Our artisans excel in skill, and our discoveries rival the genius of the world. I speak of all this as sober truth, which should call forth the nation's gratitude, and be matter of just pride.

This glorious land is ours—let it never be divided. Let no profane hand ever "remove the ancient landmarks." Let not an inch of it ever be conceded to rebellion. The politicians of Europe tell us that our "lines" embrace too much territory, that the magnitude of the great Republic endangers the peace of the world, that it is necessary that we should be weakened by divisions and subdivisions. The governments of the old world may find out that their peace may not be secured by their intermeddling with our affairs, and the best way to preserve the peace of the world is for them to let us alone. As to gratifying their wishes for a *southern slaveholding confederacy*, it may be done when the patriotism of the nation dies out—never before. The integrity of the whole country is the motto of every loyal citizen, and will continue to be, in storm and in sunshine, in light and in darkness, in weal and in woe.

We have a heritage of free institutions.

Our fathers, and the God of our fathers, bequeathed to us civil and religious liberty. The "inalienable right of life, liberty, and the pursuit of happiness" is accorded to all who have not forfeited these inestimable blessings by crime. The only other exception to the rule is southern slavery, and this great nuisance is rapidly being abated, and there is no reasonable doubt but it will soon be utterly extinct. Civil and religious liberty is the natural birthright of every human being, and that right is enjoyed here to a greater extent, and with fewer exceptions, than in any nation upon the globe.

Liberty of conscience and of worship is an invaluable privilege. Here no man's conscience is restricted. Every one may select his own mode of worshiping God. If his professed worship does not infringe upon the rights of other individuals or the peace of society, or violate the laws of public morals, he is left to worship God "under his own vine and fig-tree, and there is none to molest or make him afraid."

Our system of education is Christian without being sectarian. The temple of knowledge is open to all, not excepting the poorest of the people. None are necessarily ignorant of anything which is necessary to make the useful citizen. The rich are obliged to help educate the poor, and to assist in the improvement of the masses; thus contributing to the happiness and usefulness of the people, and to the greater security of life and property.

We have the heritage of a true Church. It is a New Testament Church. The effete institutions which claim to be the only true Churches stand upon a traditionary succession. It is claimed that these Churches were founded by some apostle, and are administered by his lineal successors, and they are the divinely-appointed channels of salvation. It need not be made a question whether Churches were founded by the apostles at Rome, at Jerusalem, at Antioch, at Corinth, at Alexandria, and many other places. The question is, whether those same Churches are still alive. The question who originally founded a Church is not of so much importance as the question whether it is still "upon the foundation of the apostles and prophets, Jesus Christ himself being the chief corner-stone." Tradition is variable, doubtful, and often self-contradictory; but Scripture is uniform, truthful, and always consistent. A Church leaning upon Christ as the chief corner-stone, with the open Bible in her hand, proclaiming "to the law and to the testimony, if they speak not according to this word it is because there is no light in them," is a biblical Church, and consequently a true Church of Christ. The visible Church of Christ is a "congregation of faithful men, or of true believers, in which the pure word of God is preached, and the sacraments duly administered, according to Christ's ordinance, in all those things which of necessity are requisite to the same." Such a Church we have, embracing all the *faithful* of all evangelical denominations.

It is a spiritual Church.

A pure Church is not corrupted by traditions, superstitions, or will worship. It is baptized with the Holy Ghost, and is thoroughly alive. The Spirit of God lives in it and animates it. Such a Church is the Church of the Reformation. It is full of puritanic fire, and cherishes the old puritanic morality and strictness.

It is alleged in certain quarters that Puritanism is fanaticism, cant, and hypocrisy. No greater slander was ever uttered. Puritanism is a love of New-Testament order, a repudiation of all foreign mixtures with the Gospel, the spirit of rational liberty, and a recognition of the natural equality of men. The fact that the men of the Puritan stock hate slavery, and pray for universal emancipation, has brought this form of faith into great contempt at the South. No form of Christianity will pass current there but that which holds in fellowship "the peculiar institution."

We have a free Church, untrammeled by alliances with the State.

The Church asks of the State simple protection, and in return she promises true allegiance and earnest support. A true Christian cannot be an enemy to the government which gives him protection in the exercise of the freedom of conscience. The Master he serves commands him to "render to Cesar the things which are Cesar's, and to God the things that are God's," and he can no more mistake the first of these precepts than he can violate the second.

Leave to the Church an open field and unrestricted liberty, and she will win her way to universal empire. For "the kingdom, and the dominion, and the greatness of the kingdom under the whole heaven shall be given to the people of the saints of the Most High, whose kingdom is an everlasting kingdom, and all dominions shall serve and obey him." Dan. vii, 27.

I have said the Church will render obedience for protection, but I would not by this intimate that she will turn rebel when she is not protected. It was under the most tyrannical rule that St. Paul issued that noteworthy precept, "Let every soul be subject to the higher power." Under ordinary contingencies there can be no such thing as a *Christian rebel*. Those who were our Christian brethren at the South, who have entered into the spirit of the great rebellion, we are obliged to repudiate as apostates from the faith and practices of the Gospel.

" The lines are fallen unto me in pleasant places; yea, I have a goodly heritage." The hallowed scenes which the Christian passes through, and which continue to live in his memory, associated with the Church, give power and reality to these words. He remembers the day of his espousal to Christ, recollects the songs of Zion, the fervent prayers, and the earnest, faithful sermons to which he has listened, and exclaims with the Prophet, "How goodly are thy tents, O Jacob, and thy tabernacles, O Israel!" To a soldier in the army, to a sailor at sea, to a prisoner in a loathsome dungeon, how precious appears the heritage which we enjoy. Nothing more strongly marks the estimation in which David held the sacred courts of the Lord's house than his longings for them after a brief absence in the time of Absalom's rebellion. He says, "As the hart panteth after the water brooks, so panteth my soul after thee, O God. My soul longeth, yea, even fainteth for the courts of the Lord." So many blessings, so much sweet communion with the saints, so many powerful demonstrations of truth, so many conversions, such overwhelming showers of salvation, are associated with the Church of God, that to the pious soul it seems very near heaven.

The American Church commends herself to the American people. She is comprehensive, progressive, and effective. She is a power in the earth. She not only has a mission here at home, but she extends her benevolence to foreign lands. Her sympathies, like the waves of the ocean, roll on until they reach the most distant shores. The Churches are "the bulwarks of our land," and are entitled to the confidence of all who seek the highest prosperity of the country and the permanency of our free institutions. The American Church has a perfect adaptation to the breadth and progress of the American Republic. Her missionary spirit impels her toward the setting sun. She is essentially aggressive, and actually keeps pace with the tide of emigration westward, offering salvation to the hardy emigrant on the Rocky Mountain slope and the Pacific coast. She seeks the Indian in the western wilds, and the African in the southern swamps. She has trophies gathered from every locality of our broad land, and every nationality of which its heterogeneous population is composed. Let us then sing with Dr. Dwight:

"I love thy Church, O God!
Her walls before thee stand,
Dear as the apple of thine eye,
And graven on thy hand."

What a government have we! How free, how just, how strong! Who would prefer the upstart despotism of Jefferson Davis, or the weak republics of Central America? We are now contending against a malignant usurpation, secretly encouraged by England and France, and possessed of vast resources. The administration is engaged in the most gigantic civil war that history records, and it has neither degenerated into tyranny, nor failed to maintain itself through weakness. To-day it stands out before the gaze of the world a monument of the wisdom, justice, adaptation, and strength of a well-balanced popular government. By however much the government has been tried in the furnace of affliction, by so much the true patriot cleaves to it, and pledges in its defense his life, his fortune, and his sacred honor. His inmost soul is in harmony with the stirring popular song:

> "Rally round the flag, boys,
> Spread it to the breeze,
> Shouting the battle-cry of freedom."

Let tyrants rage, and anarchists gnash their teeth. God will avenge our wrongs, and our glorious flag will continue to wave over the land of the free and the home of the brave.

What free citizen of this great Republic does not feel that he has reason to thank God for his country. Let him travel in other countries; for instance, through the German States, and have his passport demanded half a dozen times in a day. Then let him return home and travel from Maine to New Orleans, up the father of waters to St. Paul, then let him cross the plains to California, then visit Oregon and the partially settled territories on the eastern and western slopes of the Rocky Mountains, and then let him return to his home in the east, and recollect that he has traveled for thousands of miles, and has not crossed the boundaries of his own country and has not once been asked for his passport; what must be his admiration of the real sublimity of this great Republic? Would he wish it cut up into petty independencies? Would he not be willing to make large sacrifices, and to strike heavy blows, and endure the dangers of the camp, and the privations of the prison, and expose himself to death itself, rather than see this grand heritage dismembered? Let that tongue be palsied that does not shout in the highest key, "Long live the glorious Union!"

The "heritage," then, which God has given the American people, embracing all the peoples who come to this land to find a home, comprehends a country almost boundless in extent and wealth, a government founded upon popular rights, and a Church of heaven's own appointment. A glorious inheritance!

> "My country! 'tis of thee,
> Sweet land of liberty,
>   Of thee I sing:
> Land where my fathers died,
> Land of the pilgrim's pride,
> From every mountain side
>   Let freedom ring.
>
> "My native country! thee,
> Land of the noble free,
>   Thy name I love;
> I love thy rocks and rills,
> Thy woods and templed hills:
> My heart with rapture thrills
>   Like that above.
>
> "Our fathers' God! to thee,
> Author of liberty!
>   To thee we sing:
> Long may our land be bright
> With freedom's holy light:
> Protect us by thy might,
>   Great God, our King!"

II.
OBEDIENCE TO CIVIL GOVERNMENT.

Let every soul be subject unto the higher powers. For there is no power but of God: the powers that be are ordained of God. Whosoever therefore resisteth the power, resisteth the ordinance of God: and they that resist shall receive to themselves damnation. For rulers are not a terror to good works, but to the evil. Wilt thou then not be afraid of the power? Do that which is good, and thou shalt have praise of the same. For he is the minister of God to thee for good. But if thou do that which is evil, be afraid: for he beareth not the sword in vain: for he is the minister of God, a revenger to execute wrath upon him that doeth evil. Wherefore ye must needs be subject, not only for wrath, but also for conscience' sake. For, for this cause pay ye tribute also: for they are God's ministers, attending continually upon this very thing.—Rom. xiii, 1–6.

The origin and authority of civil government are at all times important subjects of study, but especially so at the present time. And as the apostle treats this subject specifically, it should not be ignored by the pulpit. No duty is more explicitly enforced than that of obedience to the civil authority, and yet none is more lightly cast off.

The recklessness, or the levity with which our civil obligations are often treated may be the evil fruit of infidelity, but doubtless it is often the result of defective education, or of thoughtlessness. When it results from the latter cause, instruction and warning may be the means of reformation; but when it is the fruit of utter depravity, the case may be considered hopeless.

My object in the present discourse shall be to arouse the conscience and to stimulate the activities of such as retain a reverence for God's word, but have given no special attention to the moral and theological bearings of this great question.

I understand the text to assert,

That civil government is a divine institution—"The powers that be are ordained of God."

Any form of government which secures the rights of the governed is covered by the apostolic rule. The writers of the New Testament give preference to no specific form of government; but while they recognize the authority of government in general, leave the particular details to the discretion of legislators, or of the people.

Government always has for its object, justice, the protection of individual rights, and the preservation of the public peace. Some forms of government are better adapted to these ends than others; but an imperfect government is vastly better than none. The thing itself and the ends it proposes are from God, and the imperfections of its forms do by no means vitiate its authority.

This principle cannot be made to cover such abuses of civil authority as violate the principles of natural law and natural justice. The ends of government are sometimes utterly subverted by a corrupt administration, and in such cases the divine sanction of government is no defense. The immorality and the cruelties of Nero and Cesar Borgia were simply abuses of power, and not the legitimate exercise of the functions of government.

Government is a coercive power. It holds "the sword." It is "a revenger to execute wrath upon him that doeth evil."

Government of necessity is invested with the moral right of its own protection, preservation, and perpetuity. This right necessarily implies the right of coercion. The end of administration is the enforcement of obedience to law. This end is accomplished by the infliction of pains and penalties, and is entirely secured in the proportion in which the penalties of violated law are uniform and certain consequences of crime. If the minister of justice "beareth not the sword in vain," if there is no compromising the claims of law, nor escape from its penalties, government is then a mighty power for good.

The supposition of a civil government without the power of coercion is an absurdity upon the face of it; and coercion implies the power of appropriate punishment—in extreme cases the power of life and death. Sacred as human life is, it may be taken when necessary for the preservation of the government or the public safety. It is a fearful alternative to take human life, but there are alternatives still more fearful. It would be a terrible thing to take the life of a midnight assassin in the act of breaking into your house; but it would be a greater evil to lose your life and to have your wife and children murdered. The police of a city would be justified in shooting down a gang of robbers who should rush upon defenseless citizens in the quiet and helplessness of their nightly slumbers. A nation is justified in taking up the sword and entering the field of deadly strife when invaded by a foreign foe or by bands of rebels. War is not to be compared with the loss of liberty nor the annihilation of a nationality.

All subjects and citizens are under the most solemn obligations to submit to the civil authority. "Let every soul be subject unto the higher powers."

Subjection or obedience to law is necessary to the existence of government, and it is but reasonable that we should be subject to the power that gives us protection. If law is set at naught, it loses its power of protection and leaves the community in the condition of anarchy. "Resisting the power" is "resisting the ordinance of God." Rebellion against a legitimate government is rebellion against God, and a high crime. A Christian cannot be, in the true sense of the term, a rebel, nor can a rebel be a Christian. An individual is indeed justified in refusing obedience to a law which is plainly contrary to the divine law. He may say with the apostles in a certain case, "Whether it is right to obey man rather than God, judge ye." If he is restrained by his conscience, he is bound to refuse obedience, and, if need be, suffer martyrdom.

Again, when a government tramples upon the rights of the governed, and becomes intolerably oppressive, and there remains no other mode of redress, the people may resort to revolution. The resistance of the American colonies to British oppression we deem a legitimate assertion of their natural rights. That admirable bill of rights, the Declaration of American Independence, has commanded the respect of all civilized nations, and will be admired through all succeeding ages. There we have laid down the true grounds upon which a people may throw off despotic rule and fall back upon their natural rights. In such cases successful resistance becomes revolution, and revolution involves the necessity of reconstruction. Here is a clear exception to the obligation of obedience to the civil power, but it is altogether a different case from acts of treason and rebellion against a just government, where all grievances may be redressed in an orderly manner, under constitutional provisions, and the rights of every man, every class of men and section, may be maintained by law.

In a representative government like ours, it is indeed difficult to conceive of a case in which the redress of grievances is beyond the reach of law, and where, consequently, rebellion would be justifiable. In all the cases which may be rationally supposed, resistance to the constitutional authorities would be a high crime against God and against society.

We have seen the apostolic rule; we next proceed to consider its high sanctions. "Not only for wrath but for conscience' sake." "Do that which is good and thou shalt have praise of the same.". "And they that resist shall receive to themselves damnation."

We gather from the language of the apostle a threefold motive to obedience.

The *first* I shall notice is the approbation of conscience. This implies the approbation of our better judgment. Enlightened and unbiased conscience is God's witness, and bears testimony to the truth. When biased by education, interest, or passion, men lose the benefit of this clear light, and often become so blinded as to put evil for good and good for evil. Hence the Saviour's caution: "Take heed that the light that is in you be not darkness." In this perverted state of the conscience men often commit the worst crimes in the name of religion, and even mutter prayers while imbruing their hands in the blood of their brothers. Saul verily thought that he did God service when he persecuted the Church; but when the light of God shone upon him he saw his error. It is an enlightened and purified conscience which bears true testimony: and such a conscience always approves of obedience to law, and makes the faithful Christian citizen.

Secondly. Duty to the civil authority receives the approbation of enlightened public sentiment. "Do that which is good, and thou shalt have praise of the same."

The approbation of the public is sought as a good thing; but the approbation of men in high positions is especially desirable. None are so well prepared to appreciate the loyalty of the worthy citizen as the ruler who feels his responsibility as a "minister of God for good." Fidelity to the state, in his eye, is something more than a simple matter of expediency; it is a religious duty, and is indispensable to the good citizen. To the loyal citizen he looks for support in the execution of the laws, to him he accords his confidence, and to him he renders the meed of his highest praise.

Thirdly. The "avenger" shall pursue the track of the disloyal and the disturber of the public peace. He shall be surrendered to the sword of the minister of justice, who is divinely appointed to cut off capital offenders. In addition to this, a fearful retribution awaits him hereafter; for such "shall receive to themselves damnation." A reckoning of fearful significance awaits the disturbers of public order. The engines of divine power will be set in motion against them, and a storm of divine indignation will break upon their heads.

Such is the Pauline doctrine upon the subject of obedience to civil rulers, and such are the sanctions by which it is enforced. In the next place I shall proceed to make an application of the teachings of the apostle to existing national affairs.

This government is now contending with a formidable rebellion. Several states have professedly seceded and organized a confederation; have seized a vast amount of public property, and levied war against the legitimate government. Vast armies are now in the field upon both sides. Numbers are engaged on each side who profess to be Christians. The question with every man who reverences the Bible should be, What is the morality of this movement of the rebellious states? Is the biblical rule which requires obedience to the civil authority applicable to this case? If the present rebellion is such an instance of "resisting the power" as the apostle supposes, no motives of ambition, policy, or interest can either justify it, or in the least mitigate the guilt of its leaders and promoters. And I take it upon me to prove that the seceding states are guilty of the very crime which the apostle condemns.

The Constitution and government of the United States were organized by our fathers in an orderly manner, and adopted by the several states. The Constitution and the federal laws are paramount law to the people. The United States constitute one government. The motto originally adopted was "*E Pluribus Unum,*" which truly expresses not a mere theory, but a fact.

Now it is against this government that a portion of the United States are in open rebellion. Are they not "resisting the power?" To this question there can be but one answer. A justification, however, is set up; and that is, that the federal government has usurped unconstitutional powers and grievously oppressed the southern states; that, under the circumstances, they are excepted from the general rule; that it is a case in which the governed have the right of resistance, and may resort to revolution. Let us hear them patiently:

1. They say that the Northern states are made up of abolitionists, who are eternally denouncing slavery. Admitting all this, what then? Are not freedom of thought, liberty of speech, and the freedom of the press, essential to a free government? Are they not conferred by the Constitution and the laws framed by our fathers? Supposing we of the North have embraced wrong views of human rights, and have talked and published too much upon the subject, is this sufficient cause for breaking up the whole system of the government? We are opposed to human slavery, and so were the fathers of the government; and what of all that? Has our talk, our folly, if you please to have it so, oppressed the South, or so wrecked the Constitution that it may now be repudiated by the slave states? Southern slaveholders have talked too,

and talked foolishly enough; but none of the Northern states has ever thought of seceding, and breaking up the government on that account. Fanatics as we are accused of being, we have not yet reached such a pitch of madness as that:

2. It is alleged that several of the free states have refused to carry out the Fugitive Slave Law, and in contravention of the provisions of the Constitution have aided slaves in their flight to Canada, and have enacted Personal Liberty laws for the protection of fugitives. Much is said on these points with very little reason. Fugitive slaves have been surrendered under the fugitive law from most of the free states, and the Personal Liberty laws of the states where such exist were enacted to prevent the kidnapping of free persons of color. And if any of them contravene the provisions of the Constitution, they may be set aside by the Supreme Court of the United States. For these alleged violations of Southern rights there are ample remedies provided, to which the Southern people might resort were they disposed so to do. A majority of the judges of the Federal Court have long been in favor of what is called *Southern rights*, and, as is evident in the decision of the Dred Scott case, have not been indisposed to favor the South as far as possible.

3. It is made a grave matter of complaint that the representatives in Congress from the free states are opposed to the admission of any more slave states into

the Union, and wish to exclude slavery from the free territories. Even so. And is not this a fair subject of debate? Does the Constitution forbid this opposition to the desires of the South to extend the area of slavery? What constitutional right has slavery in the territories, or what right of indefinite extension? Should Congress, by a majority of votes, say to slavery, "Hitherto shalt thou come, and no further, and here shall thy proud waves be stayed," what provisions of the federal compact would thereby be violated? Clearly there is nothing in any of these allegations to justify or even in the slightest degree palliate rebellion. Here is no oppression, no invasion of Southern rights; and there is no possibility of grievances for which a remedy is not provided in the Constitution and the laws.

What, then, is the real occasion of this dreadful outbreak?

We must not ignore another grievance, and that is, that the people have elected a "black republican" president! Well, had not the free electors of the United States a right to elect whom they pleased? Must the majority submit to the dictation of the minority in selecting a president? There was nothing in the character or precedents of Mr. Lincoln which threatened Southern rights, no overt act to be complained of. He is not allowed so much as to enter upon the duties of his office before the South inaugurates rebellion. *O tempora! O mores!*

The real cause of this rebellion, and the philosophy of the whole movement, are to be found in the simple fact that the free states have the long arm of the lever, and have finally made up their minds not to be dictated to and governed by a minority. Southern politicians, who have hitherto controlled the government by wire-pulling and chicanery, have come to the conclusion that their game is played out, and that henceforth their numbers and the justice of their cause are to be the measure of their power, and hence they pause, secede, and set up for themselves. They were in a fair way to lose control of the government and the spoils of office, and could not brook it. Now, forsooth, the poor, abused, oppressed, insulted South strikes for freedom and justice, takes up arms, and appeals to the God of battles to maintain the right! They cry aloud for vengeance; they pray for help, and march to the field of deadly strife to redeem their injured honor!

Is not this a grand farce? Before the civilized world, under the light of the nineteenth century, and before high Heaven, these men openly rebel against the best government that ever was constituted since the world began, for no good reason whatever! This is a stupendous crime.

I take the position that armed resistance to an armed rebellion is right, and that it is the solemn duty of the government.

If the civil power "bears not the sword in vain,"

here is an occasion for its being drawn from the scabbard. The war on the part of the government is a necessary and a righteous war, one for whose success a Christian may devoutly pray to a God who loves justice and punishes outrageous wickedness. It is strictly a defensive war. It is for the defense of the public property, the defense of the capital, the defense of the Constitution and the laws, the defense of the rights of the people, the defense of our nationality. It is a war for a government against anarchy; a war for freedom against usurpation and despotism. If government has a divine commission to protect itself, and protect the weak and the helpless against oppression and despotic rule, the government of the United States is bound to oppose force to force, and to crush out this foul spirit of rebellion. It is a war of civilization against barbarism, of liberty against slavery, of order against confusion, of right against wrong. If ever the sword was drawn in a holy cause, it is so in the present war of the United States government against the great southern rebellion.

The crimes of the rebels against the government are most flagrant—their insolence is beyond endurance.

What are the issues between the parties? The government has been over-indulgent to the South. She has had an undue proportion of its patronage, and an unreasonable amount of special legislation for her benefit. All the legislation of Congress on the subject of slavery has been for its protection. In this the convictions of the North have often been violated and her conscience sorely wounded. All this we have borne with as good a grace as possible. Southern politicians in the halls of Congress have been overbearing, insulting, ruffianly, and amid all these provocations they have been endured. They have robbed the public treasury, stripped the government of its arms and munitions of war, and, hurling defiance in its teeth, have inaugurated rebellion.

More recently, the southern rebels have insulted the national flag, taken forcible possession of our forts, arsenals, mints, and government vessels; and, to cap the climax of their crimes against civilization, their pretended government has authorized a system of *piracy* on our commerce upon the highway of nations. What more can they do to characterize themselves as a huge band of brigands and outlaws? This grand scheme of rebellion and wholesale plunder has been years maturing, and has the aggravation of being a matter of cool deliberation. The worst passions have been enlisted, but the final action has been the result of malice aforethought.

This war is sure to result in the destruction and overthrow of the rebels.

God is against them. They "resist the ordinance of God, and shall receive to themselves damnation." Their controversy is with God, and he will judge them. If our government has so grievously offended that it is deemed unworthy to be the instrument of Divine vengeance, some other instrumentality will be employed to confound their counsels, scatter their forces, and wind up their career of wickedness and shame. The lightnings of Divine indignation will shiver them, and the fierce storms of resistless power will scatter them to the winds of heaven. Should the rebellion for a time be attended with success, it will nevertheless meet with ultimate defeat. Partial triumph will only make final ruin more complete and overwhelming.

It is a fearful reckoning that awaits the usurpers and petty despots of the South when they shall pass from the present scene of things to eternal retribution. The violence they employ, the blood they shed, the hearts they break, the tide of woe they drive over the land, the anguish of the dying upon the battlefield, the tears and groans of helpless widows and orphans, the voice of "lamentation and mourning and woe" from mothers "mourning for their children and refusing to be comforted because they are not," shall bring down upon them a storm of vengeance. That vengeance will surely come. "They have sown the wind, and they shall reap the whirlwind." "They shall receive to themselves damnation." What waves of sorrow, remorse, and shame shall come back upon the actors in this dreadful tragedy it is not for us now to know. We leave them in the hands of eternal justice, assured that a righteous retribution will finally overtake them. Their sins have darkened the heavens and made the earth tremble, and their punishment will be a warning to traitors and rebels in all after ages. They have made a page of history which they will ere long wish to blot, but which will stand against them, and will be the handwriting upon the wall which will make their knees smite together. O that they might pause where they are, before the cup of their iniquity is quite filled! As unhappy men, we pray for them; we pity them as poor wretched sinners; but we must meet them upon the ensanguined field as *enemies*, with sharp steel, whistling bullets, and thundering cannon. A fearful alternative this, but not so great an evil as slavery, the loss of nationality, and a retrogression of Christian civilization back into the dark ages.

Fellow-citizens, while southern traitors resist "the higher powers," let us obey and *fight!* yes, *fight bravely—fight like Christian heroes*, and may God give us the victory! Amen.

III.

THE SIGNS OF THE TIMES.

O YE HYPOCRITES, YE CAN DISCERN THE FACE OF THE SKY, BUT CAN YE NOT DISCERN THE SIGNS OF THE TIMES?—Matt. xvi, 3.

IT seems to be assumed by the Saviour that it is easy to discern the signs of the times; much easier than to understand, from the appearances in the heavens, the probabilities of storm or of sunshine. Some appearances in the face of the sky are prognostics of fair weather, others of foul weather. These signs may require some study and observation; yet we may learn to discern them. Why do we not understand the more palpable indications in the moral heavens? Is it not because of some defect in our spiritual vision? The terrible epithet "hypocrite" here implies that there is some false pretension in the matter. The point of the falsehood, in this case, may be the profession of inability to discern the signs which Providence displays of coming events, or of the present condition of things, and in the demand for some miraculous revelation. The face of the sky is more enigmatical and doubtful than these times. You understand the indications of the more difficult, and how is it that you do not understand the foreshadowings of that which is even plainer, but must have a sign from heaven?

We shall take occasion, from this text, to indicate the signs which loom up in the present condition and the future prospects of the Church and the world.

Mark the civil and political condition of our own country.

There are unmistakable signs of great depravity.

The present rebellion is an evidence of the corruption of the national heart. How could it have been matured, and have reached its present gigantic proportions, without a deep and widespread sympathy in the country? How could the rebels in the cabinet and in Congress ever have dared to broach their heresies, and to commit the overt act of treason, but for an idea that the nation was corrupt, and that the patriotism of the olden time had forsaken us, or had become weak and sickly? Unprincipled themselves, they judged that a large portion of the people were like themselves; and the state of political morality warranted the conclusion not only that the Union could be dissolved and the nation broken to pieces, but that they could forswear themselves, and rob, plunder, and murder, on the most gigantic scale, in the name of liberty and justice. Sin is never so daring when it is not warmed into life by the sympathy of numbers.

The extreme corruption of party politics in the

country is moreover evident from the rancor with which political discussions are conducted, and the villainous measures which are resorted to in order to gain and maintain the ascendancy of a party. Falsehood and slander, buying and selling votes, and flattering and fooling the ignorant, especially foreigners, are the common tactics of professional politicians. The abominable maxim that "all is fair in politics" has been practiced upon by all political parties, and the popular mind has become debased by the lies of unprincipled party hacks.

Undoubtedly some will charge me with preaching politics instead of the Gospel. I do not intend any such thing. I claim the right, as a minister of Christ, to bear a faithful testimony against wickedness wherever found. The vices of trade, the vices of the professions, and the vices of politicians as well, are legitimate objects of stricture from the pulpit. When the watchmen become such "dumb dogs" that they cannot or dare not sound the note of alarm when the simple are liable to be deceived, and the masses to be corrupted by the trickery of politicians, both the State and the Church will become demoralized.

That selfish and unprincipled men so often succeed in blinding and enslaving the people is a proof that the people need more information and independence.

The success of a republican government must ever depend upon the intellectual and moral elevation of the masses. In theory we govern ourselves. All are sovereigns. We make our decisions at the ballot box. The man who goes to the polls an *unintelligent tool* is not fit to exercise the high functions of a voter. A simple story will illustrate the point: At the battle of Antietam a Union soldier was deprived of his eyesight by a ball which crossed the bridge of his nose. He wished to get away from the bloody field, but could not see his way, and no help came. He heard a poor fellow, who was wounded, moaning not far away. He called to him, and, crawling to him on his hands and knees, found him to be a rebel, and to be wounded in one of his legs. "Well," said he, "you want to get off of the field, and so do I. You can see, can you?" "Yes, I can see, but I can't walk." "Well," said the Yankee, "I can walk, but can't see; now I will take you on my back, and you shall tell me where to go." The blind Yankee took the lame rebel upon his back and went on until he found himself in a rebel colonel's tent! Now it was the poor Yankee's misfortune, not his fault, that he came into the power of the enemy. But he who allows these limping politicians to fasten themselves upon his back, and put both hands over his eyes, will go to certain destruction, and will be a voluntary victim of their wiles. There are enough of this sort who desire the stalwart laboring classes to carry them into office. They fasten themselves upon their dupes, saying, "You must have no eyes of your own. I will tell you where to go." On they go with their precious burdens until they bring them in safety to their desired place of rest, and then they are left to shift for themselves until another emergency arises. This is a humiliating picture, and God only knows where this vicious policy is to terminate.

There are signs of immense resources in the country.

The expenses of the present war have been immense, and yet there are no signs of exhaustion in the resources of the government. English politicians predicted that the war would soon exhaust our credit, and the "London Times" warned English capitalists not to lend us money. As yet the government has carried on the war without asking English capitalists for a penny, and the national resources have scarcely been touched. Under the blessings of heaven the nation has been growing rich for the last ten years to an unparalleled extent; as though God had been preparing her for the present fearful struggle. We have plenty, money is easy, labor is well rewarded, and so far as the means of living are concerned, scarcely any one feels the pressure of the war.

There is evidence that the nation has great power of resistance.

The rebellion took the nation by surprise. The leading cabinet officers were in sympathy with it, and the whole course of the administration was calculated to cripple the arm and palsy the heart of the nation.

The treasury was exhausted, the navy scattered to the four winds, the army distributed among the southern forts, under the command of southern officers, and the arms and munitions of war sent south. Such was the condition of things when the war broke out.

The rebellion assumed gigantic proportions, and had the sympathies of France and England, but has been withstood now into the third year. We have created a splendid navy, have raised vast armies, and have steadily gained ground upon the rebellion, until it has lost nearly one half of its territory, and is staggering to its fall. The free states have several times been invaded, but in every instance the invaders have been met and hurled back with vast losses of men and munitions of war. The capital has often been threatened, and has sometimes been in danger, but is now safe against all probable contingencies.

There are signs, which cannot be mistaken, of the downfall of the institution of slavery in this country.

The war waged by the rebels for the perpetuation of slavery is fast working its ruin. Already sentence has gone out against the great abomination. It has received its deadly wound, and will expire with the termination of the rebellion. There never was a more fatal infatuation than that which moved the slave states to rebellion. If they had designed to make a speedy end of " the peculiar institution " they could not have devised more effectual measures than to engage in open rebellion against the government. If the great traders in this stupendous wickedness had not been judicially blinded they would have foreseen what has come upon them. There is truth in the principle expressed in the old heathen maxim: "Whom the gods design to destroy they first make mad."

There is a glorious future in reserve for the poor degraded and down-trodden children of Africa. So far all the predictions of the pro-slavery party have failed. With them it was a fixed fact that the emancipation proclamation would bring on a servile insurrection; that the blacks would not make soldiers; that white men would not fight in the same army with them, and the like; all of which has been falsified by history. The signs to-day are that the African slaves of the South will constitute an important arm of the service, and that putting arms in their hands will prove to be the first step of their onward march to the condition of true manhood.

No nation has ever been subjected to a severer test, and none could have borne itself more nobly under the trial. And this she has done with a large and influential minority in stern opposition to the policy of the administration. Partially crippled by opposition at home, still the government has astonished the world with the splendor of its achievements. A greater pressure never bore on the heart of a nation, and a more majestic resistance was never made to a hostile power.

There are evident signs of the early triumph of the national cause, and a future of great prosperity.

God can make the wrath of man to praise him and restrain the remainder. He knows when to overrule and when to restrain. He is not in haste in his providential arrangements. They are often covered with the vail of uncertainty for a long time. Nations as well as individuals are often disciplined by delay, and required to walk by faith and not by sight. He reads Providence to little profit who interprets delays and partial reverses as indications of final failure. The star of hope often glimmers through stormy clouds, and a lowering sky may give place to bright sunshine.

The national firmament is brightening, and hope gilds the whole heavens. If, as the signs of the times seem to foreshadow, the gigantic rebellion with which the government is now contending shall be put down by the present administration, this result will be one of the most splendid passages in the history of the world. It will prove that republics are not necessarily weak, and that an administration constitutionally elected by the people, although opposed by a strong minority, can stand against a local rebellion of terrible power and at the same time against party factions within its own acknowledged jurisdiction.

Let us survey the nations of the old world and see what the signs of the times are there.

There are signs of corruption there.

The nations of Europe rival us in falsehood. How fearfully have they falsified all the facts which have made up the history of the present struggle! Have England and France tried to do us justice? They have refused to acknowledge our victories, or have turned them into defeats. England especially has misrepresented our generals in the conduct of the war, and charged them with crimes which they never committed; has laughed at us for fighting bloodless battles; and then has affected to weep over the wholesale slaughter and savage cruelties of our sanguine encounters. England and France both have been wanting in good faith as neutral powers. They have encouraged the rebellion; they have played into the hands of the rebels. Englishmen have helped them to a navy, and have been largely concerned in a contraband trade with their blockaded ports. So long as by agitating the subject of slavery she could create dissatisfaction at the south she was for abolition; but when the slaveholders rebelled she became the advocate of slavery, that she might help the South to achieve its independence. An ardent friend of abolition, as England always claimed to be, a slaveholding empire in the southern states to her is preferable to a mighty free republic on this side of the Atlantic. A few years ago she sent over George Thompson and others to preach up abolition, and to agitate the country on the subject of the horrors of African slavery; now she seeks to make this terrible evil perpetual. In this England seems to be inconsistent, but she is fearfully and wickedly consistent. In both cases *she seeks to promote the spirit of the rebellion at the south and effect a permanent separation of the slave states from the free states, that the great republic may no longer be a formidable rival.* A strong and prosperous republic is a greater evil in the view of English statesmen than African slavery. The daughter has grown too fast and acquired too much wealth and power to suit the old mother, hence her possessions must be divided, and constitute two weak governments instead of one strong one.

France sympathizes with England in her general policy toward us, but pursues another route to encompass the same object. Intervention in Mexico undoubtedly has for its object the limitation of the power and influence of the American Republic. France was our old ally, but is now becoming our most formidable foe. She was our friend when we were weak, but now that we have become strong she turns against us, but not until we become divided among ourselves. There is a meanness about this that French pride ought to scorn. She becomes our foe, and seeks to strike us with a fatal blow when our hands are tied and we are in a manner helpless; while we have full employment with the rebellion she assumes a threatening attitude. This is the time, says Napoleon III., to humble the pride and break the power of the fast-growing republic, and I will begin by annihilating the Monroe doctrine. This doctrine disposed of, I will watch the opportunity for striking a blow at a more vital part and bring American progress to an end.. Little comfort will come to him by his policy in the long run.

There are signs of weakness in the two great powers, to which we principally confine our remarks under this head.

The *jealousy* and *envy*, which are but poorly concealed in the English and French governments, in view of American prosperity, can originate in nothing so much as a sense of weakness in themselves. We are not jealous of those far below us, nor do we envy the weak or the degraded. It is as a competitor, a dangerous rival, that those proud nations watch us with an evil eye. Their leading papers say that united we are dangerous to the peace of the world, but divided into two hostile governments they can take care of us. An alliance with one part will enable them to manage the other. Hence they have done everything by way of encouraging the rebellion except to send armies to sustain it.

These nations are jealous of each other.

They are perpetually watching *the balance* to see where the evidence of the greatest weight concentrates. England and France went into an expensive war ostensibly to protect a weak ally, but really to prevent Russia from becoming too strong. They have an alarming sense of *lightness*, and when another power becomes a little more ponderous they fear they will go up. France and England are rival powers, but at present they are in close and intimate fellowship. The reason is, they can, by a close and intimate union, best secure their own ambitious ends. They each wish to hold in check Russia and America, an object which, singly and alone, neither of them would be able to effect. A common interest will drive together thieves and cutthroats, but when the occasion has passed they will rob and murder each other.

It is a fair question, What right has one nation to set bounds to the growth and prosperity of another? If my neighbor makes money faster than I do, have I any right to abridge his income or his power of accumulation? An individual has as much right to insist on the balance of power as a nation has; why not?

Let us survey the condition and prospects of the Church.

In comparison with the other institutions and interests in this great world the Church occupies the highest elevation. It is made up of *believers*, professedly sanctified men and women. It is the school in which we are prepared for the heavenly state. It is then a question of the highest interest, What are the signs which indicate the present status and the future progress of the Church?

First of all let us turn our eyes to Asia, the cradle of Christianity.

Although the sacred places have been trodden down by the foot of Mohammedans for a thousand years, and the old Greek literature and civilization have been nearly annihilated, a few sparks of the old Jerusalem fire are beginning to show themselves in Palestine, in Syria, in Armenia, and in Persia. India has been a field of missionary labors and missionary designs for more than forty years. The great Chinese wall is broken down, and European civilization and the missionary are there. Japan will soon be a missionary field, where the Bible will be read, Christ will be preached, and converts to Christianity—that religion hated and persecuted since the days of the Jesuit missionaries—will be multiplied like the drops of the morning. Asia will be restored. The work is progressing, and the star of hope shines gloriously in the distance.

We come next to Africa—poor, degraded, and down-trodden Africa.

Christian colonies are planted upon the southern and western coasts of the land of Ham. From the interior the Macedonian cry is heard, "Come over and help us." "Ethiopia is stretching forth her hands unto God." The enslavement of the African race, which has scattered her children over the western hemisphere, is fast being overruled by the providence of God for her Christianization and the restoration of her ancient civilization. The Christian republic of Liberia is now exerting an influence far back among her wild and wandering tribes, while Christian travelers are penetrating her vast and long-hidden and unknown center, and opening the way for the commerce of the civilized world and the spread of the Gospel. A spirit of deep and earnest inquiry is found among the tribes and petty states of the African race furthest away from European civilization. All this shows that the day of her redemption is at hand.

We next take a glance at Europe.

As we are returning from the East, we will first notice *Italy*. Rome once gave law to the world; now she is the center of a base kingdom. Italy has recently made great advances toward liberal institutions, but the temporal power of the pope is an incubus upon her heart. She is struggling to relieve herself of this intolerable burden, but is met with French bayonets. If Louis Napoleon should take his hand off from Italy she would be free in a day. That proud but weak ecclesiastic Pius IX. rules his estates not with *masses* and *groans* and *allocutions*, but through the instrumentality of a foreign police. The press, speech, and worship are made to conform to an antiquated policy and an effete system of will-worship. But the throbbings of heart among the intelligent and educated classes for liberty of conscience, of faith, and of worship, are deep and earnest, and the object of their yearnings will by and by be realized.

France is semi-infidel, professedly Catholic, but in her there is a living Protestant Church, a portion of it supported by the state and a part by the voluntary contributions of the people. Since the expulsion of the Huguenots by the revocation of the edict of Nantes, Protestants have been tolerated only for a portion of the time. Within the past century it has made substantial progress under great difficulties, and enjoys a vigorous life. With a fair chance, that professedly popish but really skeptical people would become thoroughly Protestant, if not Methodistic.

Germany is experiencing a shower of salvation, mostly the fruit of American missionary labors. The mother of the Reformation, after a long course of wandering in the mazes of rationalism, seems bidding fair to repose in evangelical Christianity. Spiritual religion is now being extensively propagated by Germans who had imbibed its spirit in America, and returned to the fatherland to spread it abroad.

Spain and *Portugal* are now as dark as in the dark ages. Building a superstitious worship upon a traditional foundation, the Bible almost entirely proscribed, the masses of course ignorant of divine truth, these are semi-heathen countries. Some mighty upheaving of the nations by and by will break the chains of civil and spiritual despotism and let light shine upon this darkness.

England, Scotland, and Ireland enjoy liberty of conscience, but the national Churches are hampered by their connection with the State. The English Church has an orthodox creed and an evangelical liturgy, but no power of discipline. Although the old English reformers maintained that "a godly discipline" is one of "the essential notes of the Church," the Church of England has lost that essential attribute of a true Church of Christ by her marriage with the State. High Churchmen have maintained that the Articles and Liturgy of the Church of England constitute an impassable barrier against heresies and schisms. The time is now within the recollection of many when Churchmen boasted that they were a unity. The denominations were divided into innumerable small bodies, but "the Church" is one, built upon the glorious foundation of her Articles, Liturgy, and Homilies; she has "One Lord, one faith, and one baptism." In this she enjoys a glorious eminence, and challenges the admiration of the world. More than all this, she has the "apostolical succession," and is secured from the danger of fatal heresies by the special promise that "the gates of hell shall not prevail against her."

This is a beautiful theory, but it has been refuted by two facts which have transpired within our own time.

But a few years since the Oxford divines commenced publishing their "Tracts for the Times," in which there was exhibited a strong leaning toward Rome. The Romish dogmas there broached were condemned by a portion of the clergy and laity, but nothing could be done authoritatively and effectually to correct these gentlemen and to remove the scandal. The majority of them remained in the Church until they became tired, and then went over to Rome at their leisure; while others, with Dr. Pusey, himself the leader in the movement, remained in the communion of the Church. Here sprang up a mighty defection despite the Thirty-nine Articles, the Liturgy, the Homilies, and the apostolical succession!

Later still a number of Church-of-England ministers commenced publishing "Essays and Reviews," which were not merely of infidel tendency, but contain the most barefaced infidelity itself. And finally one English bishop, Colenso, published a volume setting forth and vindicating these same infidel heresies! There he is; he cannot be disposed of. The scandal still remains. The most which can be done, it seems, is for a number of the orthodox bishops and clergy to advise the Right Rev. Heretic to resign his episcopal office, a thing which he stubbornly refuses to do. Bishop Colenso cannot be disturbed unless by a decision of the civil courts.

Such is the effect of the union of Church and State. Discipline is lost, and, according to the old English fathers, one essential characteristic of the Church is wholly wanting in the present Church of England.

In England, Scotland, and Ireland there are numerous bodies of evangelical Christians which maintain "a godly discipline," are orthodox in essentials, and recognize each other as a part of the family of Christ. So also in the national establishment there is an influential though not a numerous party who contend for vital godliness, and eschew the dogmas of both the High Church and infidel parties.

These various bodies are increasing in influence and strength, and there arises hope for the rising tide of evangelical religion in the British Isles, and that the English Church proper will stand in her lot in "the day of decision," when the final battle shall be fought between truth and error, sin and holiness, God and "the prince of the power of the air."

We come to the American Church.

In America we have the true theory of liberty of conscience, and of the independence of the Church from the State. Here the Church has an open field and the chance of a fair fight. She has nothing and wants nothing from the State but protection from violence, and the right of faith, of worship, and of proselytism. With this liberty, and the same protection extended to citizens generally, the Church will conquer the world.

Here the Church is *many*, but still *one*. The various evangelical denominations agree in essentials. This is the age of good feeling among the living Churches. Since the meeting of the great "Evangelical Alliance" in London, in 1846, the rancor of sectarian feeling has, in a good degree, subsided, and spiritually-minded Christians have been constantly approaching each other. That grand assemblage of living Christians in Freemason's Hall, in London, was like a great *love-feast*. All hearts were melted and ran together. A clearer evidence could not be afforded that religion is the same in all nations and among all denominations of Christians. The days I spent in this great Christian conference were among the happiest of my life, and I see the fruit of this grand demonstration of the essential unity of evangelical Christians to-day.

The evangelical Churches of the United States of America are living Churches. The unmistakable signs of life are a godly discipline, spiritual worship, soundness of faith, and a warm support of the cause of missions. They are growing, and growth is an evidence of life. They are militant, and war, or fighting, is a sign of life. The Churches of this land are encompassed with evil, but they are in general taking a bold stand against it. A great fight is going on in which all true-hearted Christians of every name are engaged. The battle rages fiercely, but the victory is sure. Already have many glorious victories been won in the name of Christ, and the signs of final and universal triumph are numerous and significant. Glorious revivals at home, and the successes of our missions abroad, are among the most striking signs of the times. The increased light, the increased activity, and the increased power of the Church, are an evidence that she is hastening on to the completion of the objects of her mission, and the consummation of her hopes. She is successfully at work at home, she is successfully at work in the army. Many are the evidences of her successes on the battle-field. The poor dying soldier-boy lisps the prayers learned in the nursery from his mother, and the labors of the Christian Commission inspire hope in the bosom of the wounded until the fields of conflict and slaughter are made vocal with prayer and praise.

The day of the regeneration is dawning. I see the genius of Christianity making the circuit of the world. She flies from mountain top to mountain top. She overshadows our fertile valleys and broad plains with her balmy wings. She crosses oceans and islands and continents, proclaiming with her clarion voice to all nations a present, a free, and a full salvation. A train follows her of peoples and nations redeemed from sin and death, who lift up their voice like the sound of ten thousand thunders, saying, *halleluiah*, *Amen*. This is the universal language of the last triumph.

It is said that two men met on the banks of the

Nile. Each saw sympathy in the countenance of the other, but they spoke different languages. They gazed at each other with intense interest. Finally one exclaimed "Halleluiah!" Instantly the other responded "Amen!" They rushed into each other's arms, and mingled their tears together. This common language will be the glorious summing up of the labors and the conflicts of the Church of Christ. We begin our halleluiahs here. Halleluiah! Let all shout halleluiah! halleluiah! Amen and amen!

IV.

STRENGTH IN THE DAY OF ADVERSITY.

IF THOU FAINT IN THE DAY OF ADVERSITY, THY STRENGTH IS SMALL.—
Prov. xxiv, 10.

DAYS of adversity are appointed to all. The most favored meet with reverses. Wise foresight and wary precaution may be employed, but adversity comes in to baffle the best concerted schemes, and to interrupt the current of general prosperity. As it is with individuals, so it is with communities. Churches and nations have their flood and their ebb tides. It is a point of great practical wisdom to know how to meet adversity. Prosperity is a test of our humility; adversity tests our faith and our patience. Many fail under each of these trials. The one who preserves his humility under a tide of successes, and the one who bears up under a series of reverses and keeps in heart, are moral heroes. Especially he who under the discipline of afflictions keeps his faith and fortitude unimpaired, exhibits true elements of greatness. On the other hand, those who fail under adversity show evident signs of weakness. That we may be armed against either failure in the time of trial let us proceed to survey

The classes of adversities to which we are liable.

One class of adversities is made up of those which befall individuals and families. The tide of prosperity is at any time liable to ebb out. "Man is born unto trouble, as the sparks fly upward." It is a part of the discipline of our probationary state. Pecuniary resources are cut off, health fails, friends sicken and die, sons, brothers, fathers, and husbands fall upon the battle-field, or waste away in hospitals. Gloom and despondency brood over the family circle, and hearths are made desolate. Opulence is succeeded by poverty and want; the full board is swept of its luxuries; plain and scanty fare, hunger and threatened starvation, show their grim visages not far in the distance. The body and the soul are subjected to the severest tests, and happy is the one who does not utterly fail in these days of adversity.

Another class of adversities is composed of such as befall the Church. The Church is in a militant state; she has her foes and her conflicts, her successes and her reverses. The Church sometimes declines in her strength, sometimes suffers from apostasies, is sometimes divided, and is sometimes persecuted. All these trials afflict and harass her individual members, and severely try their graces. It is in seasons of declension and backsliding, of schisms and persecution, that the faith of the living members of the Church in the promises of God is brought to the severest test. When persecution raged, as under the Roman emperors; when heresies were rampant, as in the days of the Nicene fathers; when schism ruled, as in the Tridentine age, the faith of God's elect was subjected to the sorest trial. When the truth of the Gospel was condemned by councils, and scouted by the dignitaries of the nominal Church, and had to conceal itself in cloisters among the lower orders of the clergy and in the cottages of the poor, "the word of the Lord was precious in those days," and the true servants of God rested wholly and only upon the promise that "the gates of hell shall not prevail" against the Church. Martyrs and confessors then bled or were sent to the stake, and none stood the test but the brave and the strong—but those who "endured as seeing Him who is invisible."

Still another class of adversities is made up of those which befall the country which we call our own. As a nation we are now suffering the calamities of a dreadful civil war. After about eighty years of almost uninterrupted prosperity, embattled hosts of men of the same nationality, language, political creed, and religious faith, are arrayed against each other in deadly conflict. Civil war is war in its worst form. A war of brothers, a war between united states, a war in a government adopted and administered by the people themselves, is an anomaly, a scandal, and a judgment. Can a greater calamity to a nation be imagined, aside from total destruction and utter annihilation? It was indeed a dark day when the slave power at the South resolved to hazard the experiment of a war of rebellion—to take up arms against the most liberal and beneficent government in the world. This was an event to try men's souls. This government had passed through many severe tests; it had been established after the terrible revolutionary struggle—had maintained a war with the most powerful nation of the world, and bravely contested her claims to supremacy upon the land and the sea, but it had never before been called to march into the field of deadly strife against its own sons. Nothing could so severely tax the national patriotism and the confidence of the people in popular government, and in the stability of free institutions, as this war of the rebellion. The bravest heart has at times been almost crushed, and the best soldier has been tempted to turn coward. The slaughtered thousands of our brave men, and the sighs of an army of widows and orphans, wafted upon every breeze, are sickening and heartrending; they are national adversities which admit of no parallel.

An aggravation of this dreadful war just now is the fact that it is traveling north, and at this moment a large army, under the command of a great general, is in Pennsylvania, and is moving upon the capital of the state. Already skirmishing parties have reached the Susquehanna, and are threatening Harrisburgh, Philadelphia, and our coal valleys at the north. The horrors of war are brought to our doors, and men's hearts are failing them for fear. Unless our army is able to put a check upon the invading force it is impossible to tell where the mischief will end.*

There is danger of fainting, or losing heart in the day of adversity.

It is adversity that tries a man's mettle. No one can tell whether he has endurance or not until he is put to hard service, nor can one's strength of heart be accurately judged of until he is tried by adversity. Whether we have the power of enduring hardness as good soldiers of Jesus Christ will appear when we come into the fight. Courage is tested by danger, patience by delays, and faith by dark dispensations. Many sustain themselves with what may seem like fortitude when no danger is near, but when the heavens lower they tremble. They stand up strong in prosperity, but in adversity they faint away. When they meet with reverses they say, as did the patriarch Jacob when he had to part with his beloved Benjamin, "all these things are against me." When the Church is in trouble they seem to think God's promise about to fail. And when the ship of state is assailed by storms they predict her utter wreck. Some minds are not equal to the slightest

---

* This discourse was delivered at Providence, Pa., on Sunday, the 5th of July, 1863, before the news of the victory at Gettysburgh, on the 3d, had arrived.

pressure, but break down under the first wave of trouble, and give up all for lost. They "faint in the day of adversity."

The cause of fainting in the day of adversity is want of strength. "If thou faint in the day of adversity thy strength is small."
Our strength is measured by adversity.
Our strength of faith.
I use the term faith here for trust or confidence. It implies confidence in God, confidence in truth, and confidence in man. No one can really have a strong soul without great confidence in God. There is uncertainty in everything else but "the everlasting arms." Here is strength for all emergencies. The soul that reposes on God is firmly fixed. "Here is solid rock while all around is sea." In all perils the language of this faith is, " God is our refuge and strength, a very present help in trouble. Therefore will not we fear, though the earth be removed, and though the mountains be carried into the midst of the sea; though the waters thereof roar and be troubled, though the mountains shake with the swelling thereof." Psa. xlvi, 1–3.

A weak faith sees no God in the storm, almost fears he has forsaken his throne and given up the affairs of the world to the sport of chance. Like Peter, they look at the boisterous waves and lose sight of Him who is able to control them, and they then begin to sink. The promises of God, his providence, history, past experiences, all have little weight; no power to inspire confidence. To those in a similar condition of mind the Saviour said, " Why are ye fearful, O ye of little faith?" He reproves weak faith as though it were a reasonable expectation that Christians should have strong faith. It is so. There are reasons enough for strong faith, and the want of it is a culpable defect.

Faith in the principles of our government is a part of our support. At the present time it is highly important that we should see something indestructible in our institutions. If we really believe in republican institutions as best suited to secure the ends of government, we ought not to give them up in despair so long as a ray of hope is left for them. Who can be so faithless as to doubt the final success of the best form of government the world ever saw? Strong faith just now in the truth, justice, and consequent permanency of our government is most important. A true Christian and patriot will never give up the principles upon which our free institutions are based while he believes them founded in truth and justice, and he will never despair of their final triumph, whatever embarrassments for the time may seem to gather around them.

Faith in man; faith in the administration of the government; faith in the army and navy, should come to our aid just now. I am among those who see good grounds for this faith. Political prejudices, the blindest and most obstinate of all prejudices, will allow of no good thing in the opposite party, and hence may see no grounds for confidence in the government. Everything to them forbodes mischief and ruin. It seems not to have entered their minds that Providence often delays and brings about its great purposes by circuitous routes. Our faith and patriotism may have to be tried more severely than they have yet been, and it may all be in harmony with the design in due time to bring us out of our present national troubles "into a large and wealthy place."

Adversity shows our strength of hope.

The want of strong or confident hope is attended with despondency, and the utter absence of it is despair. Hope keeps the heart from breaking. Any amount of present suffering of which humanity is capable can be endured while hope promises relief; but when that promise is cut off the heart sinks.

> O what were life,
> Even in the morn and summer light of joy
> Without those hopes that, like refreshing gales,
> At evening from the sea come o'er the soul,
> Breathed from the ocean of eternity!
> And O, without them who could bear the storms
> That fall in roaring blackness o'er the waters
> Of agitated life?—WILSON.

I hear some say that they have lost all hope for the country. They must be in a lamentable condition;

of course they are faint. They barely have life and breath enough to groan and complain. All their utterances are desponding; their very look is freezing.

Adversity tests our fortitude.

Fortitude is that quality of the soul by which we endure with firmness and patience the ills of life. It is a manly quality, giving dignity to the character and stability to the position and movements of one who is assailed by opposition or in peril of being jostled by adversity. History furnishes no more illustrious examples of fortitude than the heroes and heroines of our Revolutionary struggle. Our half-fed and nearly naked soldiers bore themselves with dignity and patience while their wives and daughters at home plied the wheel and the shuttle to procure food and clothing for themselves, and often chopped their own wood and carried it from the woods to their own doors in the winter to avoid freezing. All this and much more they did and suffered for liberty.

The brave Marion invited a British officer to dine with him. His dinner consisted of sweet potatoes roasted in the embers, and his table was the trunk of a fallen tree. The officer was greatly astonished, and from that time resolved to leave the British army, and finally resigned his commission, alleging as the reason that upon entering the lines of the Revolutionary army he found one of its most distinguished generals living on roots and in the utmost contentment. From what he there saw he had come to the conclusion that a people led by officers sustained by such fortitude and self-denial could not be subdued. Now let us say,

>Ay, there we stand with planted feet,
> Steadfast where those old worthies stóod;
>Upon us let the tempest beat,
> Around us swell and surge the flood;
>We fall or triumph on that spot;
>God helping us we falter not.—WHITTIER.

Are we the children of the heroes of the Revolution, and shall we "faint in the day of adversity?" If we have a tithe of the pluck of our fathers and mothers we are not now about to whimper and whine out "All is lost." No, no. There is hope. Be strong.

>The star of the unconquered will,
> He rises in my breast,
>Serene and resolute and still,
> And calm and self-possessed.
>O fear not in a world like this,
> And thou shalt know ere long;
>Know how sublime a thing it is
> To suffer and be strong.—LONGFELLOW.

The most critical period of the Revolutionary struggle was the winter of 1777-8. After the bloody battle of Brandywine Washington went with his army into winter-quarters at Valley Forge, on the Schuylkill. The winter was a very severe one, remembered and spoken of by survivors as "the hard winter." The army was deficient in supplies of food and clothing. Under these terrible circumstances the soldiers were heard to utter in tones of sadness if not of discontent, "No pay, no clothes, no provisions." The great soul of the commander-in-chief was well-nigh overwhelmed with sorrow, and it was under these circumstances that he was found on his knees in the forest earnestly pouring out his soul in prayer to God for help. Congress was tardy in its action, and aid was delayed beyond endurance. On the 16th of February Washington wrote to Gov. Clinton, " For some days past there has been little less than a famine in the camp. A part of the army has been a week without any kind of flesh, and the rest three or four days. Naked and starving as they are, we cannot enough admire the incomparable patience and fidelity of the soldiery, that they have not been, ere this, excited by their sufferings to a general mutiny and desertion." To add to the horrors of the scene, the small-pox broke out in the camp with great virulence. Many died of this dreadful malady, and many more suffered untold miseries through exposure and want of nursing. Washington deeply sympathized with his men, and shared with them in their privations; and truly, as Dr. Thatcher, one of the historians of the Revolution, says, " He rises in the midst of distress, and gains strength by misfortunes." What an iron will, what patience, what strength of heart, had Washington. Like the sturdy oak beaten by the tempest, every blast adds to its strength, and sends its roots deeper into the ground.

What examples of fortitude and endurance were the soldiers of the Revolutionary army! They did not "faint in the day of adversity." They were men of great "strength." Let these glorious heroes be our examples in these times of trial.

V.
FIERY TRIALS OF OUR FREE INSTITUTIONS.*

THE BUSH BURNED WITH FIRE, AND THE BUSH WAS NOT CONSUMED.
Exod. iii, 2.

THE burning bush was a supernatural appearance, and was symbolical both of the condition of the children of Israel in Egypt and of the Church of God in all ages.

The doctrine taught in "this great sight" is,

That there is a discipline of severe trials appointed.

That these trials are not destructive, for

God is in them.

I shall apply these doctrines to the history and the present condition of our country as furnishing reasons for thanksgiving to-day.

The first instance of severe discipline which I shall notice is the policy of the mother country in the government of her colonial possessions in America.

That policy was extremely oppressive; better suited to the condition of slaves than of free men. The colonies complained chiefly of taxation without

* Delivered in the Presbyterian Church in Scranton, Penn., on the occasion of the National Thanksgiving, Nov. 26, 1868.

representation; but they had many other serious grievances, all of which are eloquently set forth in the immortal Declaration of Independence: a Bill of Rights unrivaled in the lucid and compact manner in which it teaches the philosophy of government. The rights of the governed are here clearly set forth and vindicated, and the fact that governments are instituted for the benefit of the governed, and not for the sole advantage of governors, although then a novel doctrine, in this instrument is boldly maintained. The civil and ecclesiastical oppressions which had driven the old Puritans away to the wilds of America had created in them a strong sense of injustice and oppression, and a stern resolve to vindicate their rights. The fiery ordeal through which they had passed had disciplined them for the stern conflict which followed. England thought to school a continent of colonies in the principles of passive submission, that they might be held in vassalage and be made tributary to her wealth and overshadowing power; but, under the hand of God, she was really creating a nation. The cruel oppressions of the mother country were not crushing, for God was in them.

The next serious trial to which this country was subjected was the war of the Revolution.

The colonies were forced to the alternative of vassalage or a war of resistance. War with the parent government was dreadful, but slavery was still more dreadful, and was not to be thought of. The colonies were without an army, without munitions of war, without a navy, without money, and almost without credit. They had a conviction of the right, and courage to defend it; this was their strength and their hope. "Thrice armed is he who hath his quarrel just."

The fearful struggle commenced with the battles of Lexington and Bunker Hill. It progressed with the usual fortunes of war. Successes and reverses succeeded each other. The untrained troops of Washington, but half clad and half armed, were often brought down to the borders of despair. When the general was driven across New Jersey, and it was not certain but he would be obliged to flee across the Alleghanies, it was a dark day; but still he trusted in God and watched his opportunity. With the capture of the Hessians at Trenton the tide turned, and after a hard struggle of six years the surrender of the two armies of Burgoyne and Cornwallis opened the way for peace, based upon the acknowledgment of American independence. The arbitrament of war is at all times terrible, but in some instances it is the only alternative, and in this case it was the condition of giving birth to a nation.

The formation of the federal Constitution was the occasion of another severe trial of the patriotism and virtue of the people.

The Articles of Confederation, by which the states

were united for mutual defense, did not constitute a national government. They furnished no basis of national credit, nor a uniform system of commerce. After an experiment of seven years of peace, from 1783 to 1790, under the old order of things, the federal Constitution was adopted by a popular vote. The conflicting interests of the different states as to trade and commerce, originated parties upon the question of state rights and the provisions of the Constitution. An excise law was passed by Congress which was opposed in Western Pennsylvania. Seven thousand armed men threatened to resist the power of the general government, and actually resisted the collection of the tax. President Washington made a requisition on New Jersey, Maryland, and Virginia for fifteen thousand militia, and putting them under the command of Governor Lee of Virginia, they were marched across the Alleghany Mountains, and the insurgents were scattered without killing a man or firing a gun. Here is an instructive lesson. Promptness on the part of the chief magistrate easily quelled a rebellion. The cheapest method of dealing with rebellion is to meet it early, and with a strong hand.

President Washington seemed not to have entertained certain views of the Constitution which have been propagated in our days—that the militia of the state are only designed for the service of the state, and that the President has no authority under the

Constitution to require them to cross state lines, or to call them out for the defense of the Union. Washington knew that section 2, paragraph 1, of the Constitution declares that "the President shall be commander-in-chief of the army and navy of the United States, and of the militia of the several states when called into the actual service of the United States," and every school-boy ought to know as much. It is, indeed, humiliating to know that three out of five judges of the Supreme Court of the State of Pennsylvania seem not to be aware of any such provision in the Constitution. Verily this is a progressive age.

The Constitution underwent severe scrutiny. The interests of different classes of citizens naturally led them to different views of the provisions of this great instrument. Two great political parties grew up in the country, which contended fiercely for the ascendency, and their contests were sometimes more deeply characterized by the spirit of faction than of patriotism. Washington clearly saw the tendency of the local feelings and political strifes to the dissolution of the Union, and the destruction of the hopes of the country, and in his farewell address left us an earnest warning against those fearful evils. Well had it been if the warning had been duly heeded by the present generation.

The doctrine that each separate state is a sovereignty in itself, was maintained by the antifederal politicians of the southern states, such as Jefferson,

Randolph, and Calhoun. The South is an agricultural country, and was more naturally led to adopt the doctrine of free trade *versus* a tariff for the support of the federal government, and for the encouragement of home manufactures. They wished to sell their cotton, tobacco, and rice to European traders, and to receive their fabrics in return without the interference of the federal authority. They maintained that it was their right to do so, and any interference with this right on the part of the federal government was a usurpation, and an attempt to reduce the separate states to slavery. The antifederal party called themselves *Republicans*, while the federal party were called *Federalists*.

The conflicts between the two parties upon the above and other subjects imposed a severe test upon the federal Constitution and the union of the states under it. Under the ordering of divine Providence, however, a regard for the Constitution, and a love of the Union, became deeply fixed in the public mind, and local interests were yielding to the demands of the national welfare, until another severe trial came upon the Republic.

The war of 1812 with the mother country.

The great war between France and England, which desolated Europe, seriously interfered with the commerce of neutral powers. The United States government made earnest complaints through her representatives to both courts without receiving any satisfactory redress. At length the question of retaliatory measures was seriously entertained by the United States government. On the recommendation of President Jefferson, Congress laid a general embargo, prohibiting the exportation of all commodities from the United States. The commerce of the country was at once reduced to a coasting trade. A stagnation of business followed which spread ruin among our merchants on the seaboard, raised the price of foreign goods, and caused extensive dissatisfaction among the people. The self-denying spirit of '76 had died out, and instead of considering the embargo a necessary measure of national defense and security, it was regarded as a party measure, and judged of by its local bearings on trade and commerce. A great cry was raised against the national administration, particularly in the New England States, and a separation from the Union was sometimes spoken of as a remedy for the existing evils.

The difficulties between the United States and Great Britain seemed to mock all diplomatic efforts, until they culminated in a war between the two nations. On the 1st of June, 1812, President Madison sent a message to Congress in which the causes of complaint against the government of Great Britain, from 1803 down to that date, were ably stated, and in the conclusion of which a declaration of war was recommended as the only resort left for the vindication of the national honor.

The message was referred to the Committee on Foreign Relations. After due deliberation upon the whole subject the committee reported a bill declaring war between Great Britain and her dependencies and the United States of America. Six reasons were given in support of the measure:

1. The impressment of American citizens while sailing upon the high seas and forcing them to fight against nations in amity with the United States.

2. Violating the rights and peace of our coasts and harbors, and wantonly spilling American blood within our territorial jurisdiction.

3. Plundering our commerce on every sea, under pretended blockades, without the application of fleets to render them legal.

4. Committing numberless spoliations on our ships and commerce, under her Orders in Council of various dates.

5. Employing secret agents within the United States, with a view to subvert our government and dismember our Union.

6. Encouraging the Indian tribes to make war on the people of the United States.

The bill passed both houses, and on the 18th of June was signed by the President.

The war was opposed by the federal party on the ground that it was stimulated by sympathy with Bonaparte, was wholly unconstitutional, was more in hostility against the states on the seaboard than against the government of Great Britain, and would result in the utter ruin of the country. Politicians and newspaper editors denounced the President as a traitor to the country, and members of Congress did not hesitate to assert the right of the separate states to secede from the Union and to make open resistance to the federal government.

A convention of delegates from the states of Massachusetts, Connecticut, and Rhode Island, the counties of Cheshire and Grafton in New Hampshire, and the county of Windham, in Vermont, convened in Hartford, Conn., Dec. 15, 1814. This celebrated convention sent out a report in which the wrongs of the government were enumerated, and remedies proposed. In this report, though guarded in its language, the spirit of faction is dominant. Bitter hostility to the government and strong sympathy with Great Britain were apparent, although not so clearly developed as in some of the opposition newspapers and by political orators. Patriotism ran low, and faction ran high.

The doctrine of state rights was now the doctrine of federal New England, as it had previously been the doctrine of the southern states. This may seem to be a strange fact, but is accounted for upon the principle of human selfishness, the same principle which first gave it birth in the South. Southern politicians opposed the administration of the general government under Washington and John Adams from this stand-point, and New England opposed that of Jefferson and Madison from the same. Tariff laws, though necessary to the existence of the general government, were a tax upon the South; hence the South opposed them, and claimed the right to resist them. The war ruined the commerce of New England; hence she opposed the general government, which declared and sustained the war, and contended that it was her right to secede and rebel. How much party politics are governed by interest is apparent in more instances than one. How few are influenced by a regard for the *whole country*, and are willing to sacrifice local interest to the general good. A narrow local policy has ever been the bane of the country, and the greatest obstacle to its unity and permanent prosperity.

The fears and predictions of party politicians are usually proved groundless by the logic of events. The South grew and prospered under what they denounced as a ruinous system, and the most flagrant outrage upon their rights upon the part of the federal government; and the commerce and resources of New England outlived a war which, according to the Hartford Convention, ought to have buried them in eternal oblivion.

The party feuds and sectionalism growing out of the war were in themselves great evils, and a severe test of the strength of the Union; but God presided over the great interests of the nation, and she came out of the fiery ordeal purified and strengthened. The history of the last war with Great Britain furnishes the most ample and satisfactory proof of the power of the government to resist a foreign enemy, to struggle with domestic factions, and to prove itself indestructible. "The bush burned with fire, but the bush was not consumed," because God was in it.

The Nullification movement in the state of South Carolina, in 1832, is another instance of a severe trial of the strength of the federal government.

John C. Calhoun was the southern leader of the ultra states rights party, and headed a movement to *nullify* the tariff established by act of Congress, and to carry South Carolina out of the Union. A convention of delegates, chosen by the people of that state, passed an ordinance of nullification and secession, Nov. 24, 1832, and the state legislature sanctioned the act. Gen. Jackson, then the President of the United States, proceeded in the most prompt and energetic manner to head off what assumed every appearance of a rebellion against the general government. He sent Gen. Scott to Charleston, giving him and the collector of the port the necessary instructions to provide for the defense of the harbor and of the government property and the enforcement of the laws. The nullifiers found themselves completely forestalled, and with as good a grace as possible finally receded, for the reason that they could not proceed. The proclamation of the President is as logical and eloquent as it is patriotic, and was received with great enthusiasm everywhere, excepting in South Carolina and some of the other southern states.

Jackson had been a zealous supporter of the doctrine of state sovereignty, and had followed Jefferson in his notions of a strict construction of the language of the Constitution; yet as Jefferson had to give up his theory in the purchase of Louisiana, so Jackson was obliged to give up the same theory for the salvation of the Union. He did more than to give up the Jeffersonian theory of state rights; he proceeded to refute it, and actually took up the last plank of the old platform. After completing his argument, the sturdy old patriot proceeded to pour out a torrent of warnings and expostulations to the people of South Carolina, which are now refreshing to every patriot heart. This proclamation is a document of rare merit and of great power. If James Buchanan had adopted it, just as it is, in 1860, when South Carolina tried her hand at secession again, and had followed it up with the same energetic measures with which it was followed up by Andrew Jackson, secession would have again been stifled in its birth.

American Slavery.

The enslavement of the African race was entailed upon us by the mother country, and has been one of the greatest evils with which we have had to contend. While slavery was abolished in the eastern and northern states, in the South, by reason of the climate, the character and social habits, and the business interests of the southern people, it became established there as a permanent institution. Becoming local in its character, it finally became a subject of controversy and a source of dissension between the North and the South. As the cotton interest advanced, the value of slave labor was enhanced, and slavery was considered a source of wealth. At first the southern people endeavored to excuse slavery as a thing of necessity, but finally they came to justify it as a right. The two systems of free and slave labor are antagonistic. As free labor is most productive, the free states gradually gained upon the slave states in resources. The more rapid advance of the free states in wealth and numbers excited the envy of the South, and brought on angry collisions between the two parties in Congress and in the newspapers, which resulted in mutual dislike. The southern people were educated to despise labor, and northern congressmen and senators were often treated with the bitterest scorn, and occasionally with personal violence.

Though in the minority, southern politicians managed to hold the balance of power. Their hatred of the free North and their insolence finally became intolerable. They demanded and obtained a fugitive slave law, which was offensive to the North. They procured the repeal of the Missouri Compromise. They tried by mob violence and brute force to fasten slavery upon Kansas. Frequent raids of slave catchers into the northern and eastern states, and their dragging away into slavery respectable and well-to-do colored people, who had enjoyed the blessings of liberty for ten and even twenty years, increased the hatred of the North for the institution of slavery, and continued to widen the chasm which yawned between the two great antagonistic systems of northern freedom and southern bondage. To increase the moral sentiment of abhorrence of "the peculiar institution" at the north, scores and it may be hundreds of northern men were tarred and feathered, whipped and *hung* at the South under the pretext of their being *Abolitionists*, without the slightest evidence of any overt act of contempt for the laws of the slave states, or of offense against the peace of southern society.

The question of slavery in the territories became a source of great discontent at the South. Although Congress pretended to no right to interfere with the question in the states, yet it had the undoubted right to legislate upon it within the territories; and the northern policy was to prevent the extension of slavery, neither allowing it in the domain of the United States, nor admitting new slave states. This the South pretended to consider an infringement upon their rights, and a violation of the compromises of the Constitution; and they for a long time found sympathizers enough among northern members to enable them to maintain their position. Southern insolence had finally reached bounds beyond which northern forbearance could by no means be compelled to go. The repeal of the Missouri Compromise and the Kansas outrages had fully aroused the North; then came on a reaction against the aggressive spirit of slavery which threatened an end of its further progress.

The dissensions which arose upon these great issues were a severe trial to the Union under the federal Constitution; and it was but too evident that the southern politicians were contemplating a plan for a final separation, and the organization of an independent government. In the midst of these fearful storms the ship of state bore itself nobly, and promised to outlive the peril.

Then came the slaveholders' rebellion.

In the presidential canvass of 1860, the republican party succeeded in the election of *Abraham Lincoln*. This was made the occasion of an outbreak of the rebellious spirit of the southern slaveholders. Mr. Lincoln was elected by a majority of votes under the Constitution; but the southern chivalry said an abolitionist should never be President of the United States. South Carolina, always the first to engage in factious proceedings, inaugurated the rebellion;

and all the other slaveholding states followed, except Maryland and Delaware.

The North were not prepared for the movement—few indeed believed the thing possible. President Buchanan allowed the time from the election in November to the 4th of March, the day of the inauguration of the new president, to pass without the slightest preparations for the emergency, affording the rebels every opportunity to mature their plans and prepare for the conflict. Several of Mr. Buchanan's cabinet were in the conspiracy, and used their position to weaken the North and to strengthen the South. The Secretary of War, John B. Floyd, of Virginia, robbed the treasury, and sent from the depots of arms and ammunition at the North, large stores to the South. The rebels seized our forts, navy-yards, ships of war, revenue cutters, and mints, and indeed everything which they could make available in the struggle. Many officers, who had been educated in our military schools, joined the rebels, and turned over to them their commands. The first overt act of hostilities was committed at Charleston, by the bombardment of Fort Sumter, on the 16th of March, 1861. This act was followed by a call from the President for 75,000 volunteers for the recovery of the property of the United States and the suppression of the rebellion.

The government was totally unprepared for war upon a gigantic scale. It was almost without an army, without arms, and without money. The rebels had been long in their preparations and were fierce for the combat. Washington was threatened, and Baltimore gave unmistakable signs of disloyalty, and the whole country was thrown into the most terrible state of excitement. The patriotic feeling of the North was strong, and all seemed to anticipate universal success and an easy conquest over the rebels. The cry of "On to Richmond" was raised by newspaper editors, and echoed by the people. The disasters of Bull Run, Ball's Bluff, Fredericksburg, and Chancellorsville superinduced a considerate state of mind, and had the effect to awaken the nation to a sense of the real magnitude of the struggle in which we are engaged. These lessons were severe, but they were necessary, and it is to be hoped will be salutary.

Since last July the federal arms have been crowned with a series of successes, which it is to be hoped has inflicted upon the rebellion a deadly wound. The monster dies hard, but evidently is consuming away. May he soon expire without benefit of clergy, receive the burial of a dog, and never know a resurrection!

The problems of this terrible civil war are being solved by the logic of events. The question of finance, the disposition of the freedmen, confiscation of the property of rebels, all have had their difficulties; but the light has gradually been dawning, and difficulties melting away, until the ground for confidence seems strong, and hope of the final result bright.

The spirit of lawless violence which broke out in the city of New York was a severe test of the strength of the government.

The great riot in New York, but a few months since, had many sympathizers scattered through the free states. Threats of terminating the present administration by violence had been uttered through some of the opposition newspapers, about the time our armies were achieving their glorious victories at Gettysburg and Vicksburg; and if instead of these victories our arms had met defeat, it is impossible to tell what the consequences of the lawless spirit, which had become so rife in the country, might have been. That I am not mistaken in the indications of a purpose forcibly to resist the government will appear from the following, taken from a series of resolutions passed at a celebration in our own county July 4, 1863, and published in a newspaper thoroughly in sympathy with the proceedings of that factious meeting:

"Abraham Lincoln has nearly brought the free citizens of the North to a line of universal resistance to his mandates, which the signs all over the North plainly indicate. Multiplied wrongs, sufferings, and insults, if further attempted by the President, may bring forth their bitter fruits before the fourth day of March, 1865; and we say to the President and his cabinet, 'beware of the Ides of November;' remember the history of other usurpers and tyrants who have gone before you, or you may have use for the army of the Potomac besides that duty they are now engaged in, in order to secure you a safe conduct from the White House to Springfield, Ill. Self-preservation is nature's first law. Imbecility and rottenness are but poor safeguards for any tyrant and usurper when the people become aroused. You have sown the wind, and ominous clouds are gathering in the north, east, and west portending a coming storm."

This and much more to the same purpose in a wordy, windy report of that veritable celebration clearly indicates the spirit of the New York mob, and the anticipation of a general outbreak against the administration. Such was the condition of things when the victories of Gettysburg and Vicksburg gave new strength to the administration and relief to the country.

Through all these trials and perils our country has passed without being wrecked. She has passed through many a fiery ordeal, and as yet "the smell of fire" is scarcely upon her. It is to God's superintending providence that we owe our continued existence and our present prosperity. To him be the praise!

Fellow-citizens! we have assembled to-day, in obedience to the call of the chief magistrate of the nation, *to give thanks to God for our recent victories in the field.* It is assumed that these triumphs are a blessing, and that we owe them to the God of battles. Let us glance over the operations of our armies for the last few months. The rebel generals Lee and Jackson invaded Maryland and Pennsylvania with an army of seventy thousand men the latter part of June, and were severely defeated by Gen. Meade at Gettysburg on the third of July, and on the fourth were in full retreat. After the loss of at least twenty thousand of his men Lee fell back toward Richmond to recuperate. On the same fourth of July the rebel Gen. Pemberton surrendered Vicksburg, the key of the Mississippi, to Gen. Grant. On the eighth of July Port Hudson was surrendered to Gen. Banks. The Mississippi was now opened to New Orleans, and the rebel states severed in twain. Important victories in Arkansas and Tennessee, and the advance of Gen. Rosecranz to the borders of Georgia, are also to be taken into this account, and for the whole do we to-day, as a nation, offer devout thanksgivings to God.

There is a religious spirit in the army. Many prayers are there offered up. Multitudes of the brave men who have fallen upon the battle-field have pillowed their heads upon the bosom of Jesus as they bid adieu to earth.

Still the nation is in the fire, but is not likely to be consumed, for *God is in the fire.* Under his supervision the fire is melting away the chains of slavery, humbling and purifying the nation, and preparing her for a glorious future. The work is not yet fully accomplished. God grant that it may be "cut short in righteousness." May the American eagle, carrying the national motto, "E PLURIBUS UNUM," soar unimpeded from the Atlantic to the Pacific, and from the Canadas to the Gulf of Mexico, and in answer to the shrill cry of the mystic bird may the whole people respond, in the noble language of Webster, "Union and liberty, now and forever, one and inseparable." The shout of GOD AND LIBERTY, sent up from our high mountains and broad plains, shall be echoed back by the peoples and nationalities of the eastern hemisphere, and universal man shall be one great brotherhood.

VI.
RADICALISM.

HE THAT DASHETH IN PIECES IS COME UP BEFORE THY FACE: KEEP THE MUNITION, WATCH THE WAY, MAKE THY LOINS STRONG, FORTIFY THY POWER MIGHTILY.—Nahum ii, 1.

THE work of building up, and the work of breaking down, each has its agency and its period. If it were not for incendiaries much of this world's labor would be saved. Some periods seem to be specially characterized by systematic efforts to break up old foundations, long-established systems and usages. Revolutions which improve the condition of things are real reforms, but many changes are retrogressive, pushing society back toward barbarism, or tending to anarchy. The active working of destructive elements in the social system at the present time is apparent. *Radical reformers* are now the most dangerous enemies to real progress. Some real or supposed evil in the social system is made a reason for a wholesale destruction of its very framework. A destructive and a constructive genius are seldom found in the same mind; and hence an old fabric is often pulled down without the erection of a better one in its stead.

In this discourse I shall mark the tendency to injurious changes, and then proceed to find the remedy.

Observe the tendency to break down and destroy. There is a tendency to break down parental authority. "Children, obey your parents in all things; for this is well-pleasing to the Lord." Col. iii, 20. This is a revealed truth, which former generations of parents enforced and children respected. In the good old times the father was the head of his family, and the children revered his authority. Now, in too many instances, the strict old Puritan rule is denounced as arbitrary and cruel, and what is considered the more philosophical plan is that of giving children some good lessons occasionally, and then leaving them to follow their own promptings until reason corrects their childish passions and habits. The modern theory is, that children should never receive physical punishment: that would do for the barbarous ages, but is inconsistent with the refinement of the present improved condition of society. Solomon said, "He that spareth his rod hateth his son;" and St. Paul said, "We have had fathers of our flesh, which corrected us, and we gave them reverence." Those are teachers of the ancient schools, and will hardly bear criticism in these days. Now it seems to be seriously believed that if you punish a disobedient child it makes him worse, but leave him to his own wont and he will correct himself.

I would only favor punishment, in parental discipline, as a means of maintaining authority, and of course it must always be in reason. Excessive punishment provokes resentment and generates hatred, and consequently counteracts its own ends. On the other hand, to allow downright impudence and willful disobedience to pass with impunity destroys all parental discipline. The absence of early restraint and suitable punishments is likely to result in a harvest of infamy. The little urchin who breaks crockery and pounds his head on the floor, and is pacified with sugar, will be likely at length to curse his father and his mother, and to trample them under foot. Many sad specimens are seen in these days of filial ingratitude, which can only be accounted for upon the ground of the inefficiency of family discipline. Young people are too often brought up in idleness, and indulged until their habits of extravagance become unendurable, and they are utterly spoiled for any useful or honorable position in society. Labor is becoming disreputable. Our fathers were apprenticed to trades, but our children must be taught to dance and read novels, have plenty of money, and time to seek their pleasure.

The same tendency to the breaking down of authority in the family is discovered in the schools of our times.

It is no unusual thing for parents to interfere with the discipline of the school. Their children, who have been pampered and spoiled at home, can scarcely brook restraint abroad. One of the greatest burdens of a teacher now arises from the irregular habits of the pupils—their aversion to order and method, and their impatience of restraint. Our schools and colleges in too many instances are used as places of recreation for idle young people—merely necessary as a gangway between childhood and manhood, or womanhood. Who takes lessons in subordination and respect for authority in the schools of our time? The teacher who is excessively indulgent is well spoken of, but the strict disciplinarian will be dubbed with some outlandish nickname, which is sure to have the prefix *old* connected with it. Then they will be talked of as *cross*, and the parents at home very soon get a horrible idea of the temper of the teacher, and come to regard their sons and daughters as veritable martyrs, whom, out of sheer humanity, they call home. Poor creatures!

Church discipline, it is to be feared, is going into neglect, if not into contempt.

Legitimate ecclesiastical authority is often branded as popish, and a godly discipline is resisted as an intolerable burden. The old strictness of living is now scarcely attempted to be enforced. A breach of Church rule is regarded as a venial offense, while the pastor who watches over his flock as he who must give an account—reproving the unruly, and lopping off dead branches—soon becomes unpopular. Turbulence and open resistance of authority in the Churches are by no means unknown; but an exceedingly weak administration, through the fear of downright rebellion, is too common. Outward and inward pressure have borne upon ecclesiastical authority until it is fast becoming nerveless; and its restoration to its original vigor and efficiency is all but hopeless.

Old formulas of faith are *dashed to pieces.*

The present age is famous for a love of novelties. Who reveres the old platforms? Who reads old authors? How many are prepared to reject a formulary or a dogma merely because it smacks of age, or has been handed down from the fathers? How common is it to hear unfledged pulpit orators expatiate upon independence of thought and the fruit of original investigation? All this is well enough in its place, and when properly qualified; but not so well when it means the rejection of the wisdom of past ages and the reckless swallowing down of every novelty which appears in these stirring times. A descendant of the Puritans will occasionally swell to a vast bulk of personal importance, and tell you that he does not ask what says Calvin or the Confession of Faith of the Westminster divines, but what is truth? In like manner you sometimes hear a disciple of Wesley vaunt his superiority to human authority by saying, I ask not what Wesley has said, but I go to St. Paul. Very well; let him, if our stripling has studied St. Paul so much more thoroughly than Wesley did, that the father of

Methodism can give him no light upon the original text of the apostle. I am not against original investigation, but I oppose the rejection of systems of doctrine and forms of faith without investigation merely because they are old.

Old Constitutions have been broken to pieces or changed until they have lost much of their original excellence.

Perhaps every state constitution has been revised, and some of them several times. The changes in them generally consist in abstracting the conservative element and replacing it with the democratic or popular principle. To instance in one thing: Our judiciary has almost universally became elective. Our judges and magistrates are now elected by the people, which none will be so bold as to deny has opened a wide door to corruption. Appeals are made to the populace for votes, and the votes are given with the expectation that such judgments will be rendered as will be palatable to the voters; and in this expectation the voters are not often disappointed. The stern old-fashioned justice of our courts would be an improvement upon the present order of things. Political judges and political magistrates are often, I will not say how often, weak in the knees, and, through fear of giving offense to political partisans, fail to render impartial justice. All feel that the old securities are gone, but many are not aware of the cause.

A conscientious regard for law and order has diminished.

In proof of the fact here assumed may be noticed the numerous instances of personal violence and breaches of the public peace. Unbridled passion often rules, while the demands of law and justice are either ignored or utterly despised. The principle of brute force and mob violence rules a numerous class, and the majesty of the laws is often utterly despised. I shall not enlarge upon this feature of the times, but will next proceed to notice the culmination of this lawless tendency.

The great southern rebellion, against which the government is now struggling, is the ripe fruit of all the corrupt principles and bad passions which have for years been taking root in American soil.

This grand incendiary experiment began in breaking down the barriers of the southern conscience. The moral obligations resting upon every citizen, as well as upon every state of the Republic, to bear true allegiance to the general government, was first repudiated by the leaders of the movement, and then the people were instructed and tempted to follow their example. Having made out a case which seemed to satisfy their minds, although it was wholly founded in falsehood, the southern politicians proceeded to the overt act of treason. The act of secession in every instance was in violation of public law, and a breach of the most sacred obligations. Its natural consequences, unrestrained, would be to dash to pieces a great and prosperous nation. The right of secession once admitted, the federal Constitution and the Union are broken up, and our nationality is gone forever. When the federal Constitution was adopted by a popular vote, an obligation was entered into, by the whole people, to bear their part in sustaining the credit of the government, and providing for its defense. The compact entered into is not only between the individuals of each state and the general government, but between the individuals of each state and those of all the other states, and also between each state and all the other states; and this compact is necessarily made for all time. If a nation at any time can dissolve itself, what basis is there for national credit? The very idea of a nation supposes adhesiveness and permanence. Thence as the separation of one state may be injustice to the others, no one state can have a right to secede without the unanimous consent of the rest.

These plain principles of law and justice were stricken down by the southern secessionists with as little compunction as they would crack their whip around the ears of a tardy slave. Having dashed to pieces the Constitution and the obligations of public justice, they next proceeded to take possession of all the property, and to destroy the power of the federal government within the bounds of the seceding states. A bloody war has been the result, which has cost the country a million of precious lives, and many millions of treasure. What an immense *dashing to pieces* of towns, railways, forts, munitions of war, ships of commerce and ships of war, armies, and human hopes has followed the march of this dire rebellion. The work of the rebels is the work of incendiaries; destruction follows in their train. The laws of civilized warfare are mocked, especially by their pirates on the high seas and their guerrilla bands, whose peculiar mission seems to be that of plunder and murder. Capturing and murdering unarmed citizens and burning unprotected towns it seems ought to be reserved for savages and barbarians; but to this species of savage warfare the chivalry descend.

Having given warning that a destructive enemy was at hand, the prophet next proceeds to advise measures of defense. Let it be observed here that no terms of peace are proposed; nothing is said about a parley or an amnesty, but only measures of defense. A war wisely planned and bravely prosecuted is counseled by the prophet.

What is the duty of the government under the circumstances?

"Keep the munition."

The fortification is to be kept. This is just what President Buchanan did not do. He left all the southern forts, with the exception of Fortress Monroe and Fort Pickens, unprotected, and one of them after another fell into the hands of the rebels. The southern members of Congress, and of the President's cabinet, warned the President that any force sent to the South would create an excitement, and bring on a collision between the United States forces and the state authorities; and either through fear of this, or some more unworthy motive, he left the rebels in possession of nearly all the defensive works at the South, which, if he had taken timely measures to secure, would have saved rivers of blood.

Thanks to the present administration, and to our able commanders of the land and naval forces, these fortifications have nearly all been recaptured, and are now being kept for the defense of the government and the country. To keep these forts vast forces and immense supplies of munitions of war are necessary. Heavy batteries, immense siege guns and men to use them, with powerful gunboats and ships of war ably manned, are also indispensable. These preparations all contemplate opposing force by force, and shedding human blood if necessary. Our war department are resolved upon keeping "the munition" at all hazards, and for this the country holds them responsible.

"Watch the way."

All the avenues through which an insidious foe may approach are to be guarded. The railroads, the highways, the rivers, the harbors, the ocean—the highway of nations—are all to be guarded with sleepless vigilance. The mode of approach through spies and traitors at home will require special attention. The government must be broad awake to every vulnerable point, and never be caught napping.

"Make thy loins strong."

The resolution or purpose of the government must be made strong. A government wants "loins," or what in modern phrase is called *back bone*. This is especially necessary in the present administration. Amid the conflict of opinions and theories, and the vast pressures which have been brought to bear upon the President and his cabinet, it has required no ordinary strength of will to pursue a consistent course of administration and to carry out measures of reform. To displace inefficient and unreliable officers in the army and the navy has been a fearful tax upon the nerve of the President. That he has nobly and promptly met every emergency is not too much to say. I may also say that as a nation we have great reason for devout gratitude that God has given us a chief magistrate and a commander of the army so well suited to the exigencies of these trying times. The opposition have by turns called him weak and strong, as the fit has taken them. On one occasion his back is weak, his knees are feeble; and on another he is a headstrong, relentless tyrant, just as the caprice of political partisanship may suggest, or the exigencies of party politics may demand. Consistency is a jewel.

"Fortify thy power mightily."

Here is authority for a sufficient force in men and a sufficient amount of arms for every occasion. A weak resistance to a strong foe is a foolish piece of policy. The case is aptly stated by Christ: "Or what king, going to make war against another king, sitteth not down first, and consulteth whether he be able with ten thousand to meet him that cometh against him with twenty thousand? Or else, while the other is yet a great way off, he sendeth an embassage, and desireth conditions of peace." The national cause has suffered more in this war for the want of an adequate force than can well be estimated. The government, fully awake to the greatness of the struggle, is now pursuing the wise policy of strengthening the army by a large number of recruits. The true economy is to have a large army. A sufficient force will save life and sooner end the war. "Fortify thy power mightily."

Here is also clearly a divine warrant for extraordinary powers to meet extraordinary emergencies. A louder outcry has been raised against the President for using the war power than for anything else. Suspending the writ of *habeas corpus* and authorizing what is called "arbitrary arrests," and denounced as despotic and without authority of law. The measures complained of are to be justified upon the ground of necessity, and, under the circumstances, they are clearly covered by the Constitution. The

Constitution admits of the suspension of the writ of habeas corpus " when, in cases of rebellion or invasion, the public safety may require it." (See art. i, sec. 9, par. 2.) Now when it is considered that there are partisan judges enough who would grant writs of habeas corpus in favor of traitors, and taking them out of the hands of the military authorities, set them at large, and thereby endanger " the public safety," what common sense is there in this croaking about depriving citizens of the privilege of the writ of habeas corpus.

As to " arbitrary arrests," there may have been some arrests made which were not expedient, although I am not now prepared to name them. Certain I am that more cases of this kind might have occurred to advantage. If all the rank traitors at the North could have been taken up and caged long ago we might have had peace. The sympathies which have been wasted upon that arch traitor Vallandigham would have been equally appropriate if they had been lavished upon Jefferson Davis or Sterling Price. Let those who have so much sympathy for the miserable traitors whom the government has had the wisdom to put where, for the time, they can do no harm, transfer a little of their sympathy from these vagabonds to our suffering, bleeding country, and thereby honor their own good sense and give proof of their patriotism.

Lastly, "fortify thy power mightily " with the divine

help and protection. No government was ever really strong without God. Our government has not been slow to acknowledge that our successes are all instances of the divine interference, and call for special thanksgiving to the Author of all good. Equally careful has the President been to admonish us that our sins have deserved all our reverses, and to call the whole people to fasting, humiliation, and prayer. Thus has our worthy chief magistrate been fortifying his power by laboring to secure the favor of the God of armies. "By my God," says David, "I can run through a troop or leap over a wall." The almighty power of God will be enlisted for the government in answer to prayer. It is for this reason that the prayers of the Churches are invoked. They have influence with God, and the President, sensible of this, says, "Blessed be God who giveth us the Churches." By God's special help may he continue to "fortify his power mightily."

VII.

THE LORD'S CONTROVERSY.

THE LORD HATH A CONTROVERSY WITH THE INHABITANTS OF THE LAND, BECAUSE THERE IS NO TRUTH, NOR MERCY, NOR KNOWLEDGE OF GOD IN THE LAND. BY SWEARING, AND LYING, AND KILLING, AND STEALING, AND COMMITTING ADULTERY, THEY BREAK OUT, AND BLOOD TOUCHETH BLOOD.—Hosea iv, 1, 2.

AN action is here brought against a guilty people. The charge is formally made and the facts produced in evidence. It is terrible that God should cause an indictment to be filed against us, and that allegations should be sustained by the most indubitable facts; but after all, an indictment and a trial are not the worst things which might occur. The cause is not decided, sentence is not yet pronounced, and the guilty party handed over to justice. There is a small space allotted for the defendant to make a plea, or to throw himself on the mercy of the court. This is the only hopeful view of the case. If the arraigned sinner were put upon the expedient of self-justification he would fail of course. There is no doubt but the charge is fully sustained, and it is not of a nature to admit of either justification or palliation. Without humiliation, confession, and forgiveness, conviction and condign punishment are absolutely certain.

We are called upon by the government to fast and pray, to humble ourselves before God for our sins, national and personal. Several such appointments have been made since the breaking out of the present civil war, the last one being attended by the extraordinary circumstance of an authorization by act of Congress. Such days should be solemnized by a devout, humble, and earnest spirit. Our prominent and aggravated offenses should be brought into remembrance and heartily bewailed.

This discourse has the advantage of having been prepared and delivered subsequent to the late national fast, (August 26, 1864,) and is retrospective. It not only contemplates the particular occasions we have as a nation for fasting, humiliation, and prayer, but also the manner in which special days of fasting have been improved, and the condition of the national heart under all the evidences of divine displeasure, and after all the efforts made to bring about the nation's repentance.

With these preliminaries I shall proceed to consider,

The grounds of the Lord's controversy.

"There is no truth, nor mercy, nor knowledge of God in the land."

The first count in the indictment is that there is no truth in the land.

Let it be first premised that although the charges

presented are in general terms they do not exclude exceptions. So that which is charged is not the absolute absence of " truth, mercy, and the knowledge of God," but a fearful deficiency of these virtues, and the general prevalence of their opposites.

Is there, then, a sad want of truth in the land? Truth is a principle which has its seat in the soul. It is simple honesty; a desire and purpose to represent everything in accordance with fact; a horror of all deception or falsehood. This virtue is to be acquired by the diligent study of facts, and a constant effort to conform to them in thought and word. A love of truth is essential to its proper development, and especially to its ripening into habits. The pursuit of truth is the most ennobling of all pursuits; a disregard of it is the most degrading of all mental conditions.

The want of truth in a community, as in an individual, is an evidence of deep-seated depravity. It is a branch of a deadly tree. The soil not friendly to truth is productive of all the corruptions and vices of the depraved human heart. The want of true sincerity advertises the want of all the virtues.

There is a want of mercy in the land.

Mercy is goodness exercised toward the suffering. The want of sympathy for the unhappy is one evidence of the want of all goodness; for wherever an object is presented mercy is the first impulse of goodness. What claim has he to goodness who can look upon suffering humanity without any bowels of compassion? No sect, no nationality is excluded from the sympathies of the really good. Not because a man was born in a certain country, or because his skin is of a particular hue, is he to be excluded from the consideration due to the common brotherhood of man. Mercy is disinterested. It is not that charity which gives "hoping to receive again," but love for the helpless and the undeserving. Purely selfish men may be bound together by common interests; but good men will feel that those unfortunate ones, who have nothing with which to repay acts of kindness, are their brothers, and have claims on them for their kind consideration.

The want of mercy is developed in the form of cold selfishness, unconcern for the woes of others, want of feeling, hard heartedness, a cold disregard of human misery.

No knowledge of God in the land.

Ignorance of God in this country is not a mere misfortune, but a crime. God has manifested himself in his works and in his word, and ignorance of him is wholly voluntary and consequently criminal. The knowledge of God referred to in the text is more an experimental than a theoretical knowledge. It is an understanding of the character of God which impresses itself upon the heart and the life; such a knowledge of his holiness as begets deep repentance; such knowledge of his truth as inspires faith; such knowledge of his goodness as calls forth love and obedience. The want of this knowledge of God is the absence of all piety; and the want of piety necessarily implies the presence of every attribute of depravity.

In this fearful indictment, then, we have added to a false heart and malice prepense the awful sin of impiety. These are kindred sins but of different bearings. A false-hearted man sins against himself, a malicious man sins against his fellow-men, and an impious man sins against God. The whole together makes up at once a rebel against God and nature.

Your attention is next invited to the facts by which the charges presented are sustained. The charges refer to the moral condition of the soul; the facts or testimony is derived from the life. The conduct of the life is the evidence of moral character. Malice is the indictable offense, but we cannot see malice or know it to exist except through the infallible signs which exhibit themselves in words and deeds. This is the ground upon which the prophet rests the cause. The charges are "no truth," "no mercy," "no knowledge of God." The proofs are "swearing," "lying," "killing," "stealing," "and committing adultery." Let us now see whether the facts contained in the specifications sustain the charges.

"Swearing." Two descriptions of the crime here alleged may be noticed, *profane* swearing and *false* swearing. Profane swearing is unnecessarily calling

God to witness, or using the name of God on trifling or common occasions. Profane swearing is so common that it, in a measure, has ceased to be witnessed with horror. The old and the young, even little children, the ignorant and the learned, the vulgar and the polite, males and females, swear profanely.

Swearing when indulged in always becomes a habit. The common swearer says he means no harm; he swears without thinking of it. That he should have formed the habit so perfectly as to commit the sin without thought is one of the most terrible aggravations of the offense, albeit it is often employed as a ground of apology for the crime. Sir Robert Boyle says: "I doubt not but that it is much easier to make most swearers proselytes than to make them converts, and a task of less difficulty to convince their judgments than to reform their practice. Customary and unnecessary swearing is so confessedly unlawful that they are ashamed to defend it that blush not to practice it; and even they renounce it in their opinions that most cherish it in their discourse." Another author truly says: "The swearer continues to swear. Tell him of his wickedness, he allows it is great, but he continues to swear on."

We need scarcely quote the divine precepts: "Thou shalt not take the name of the Lord thy God in vain," "Swear not at all," and the like, to convict the swearer. He confesses it to be both sinful and foolish, and yet he swears. There is really less excuse for it than for almost any other species of offending. It is demanded by no appetite, it satisfies no fleshly desire, yet the profane indulge in it with an apparent relish that seems to evince a strong tendency to the very wickedness of the thing. It is an instance of malice against God that might be expected in a devil, but might well be astonishing to angels and men when witnessed in a human being.

The other instance, that of perjury, is perhaps not so common as profane swearing, and yet is fearfully prevalent. Persons are often convicted of perjury; others are known to have committed the crime; still others are suspected of the guilt of false swearing. It is also worthy of remark that legal men generally, in a multitude of cases, regard the testimony offered in court with evident suspicion. This fact is in proof that those who have the best opportunity to judge in the case consider perjury a common sin. The false swearer stakes his all upon a lie. He repudiates his hope of heaven, and invokes eternal vengeance upon his soul if his tale of falsehood is not true. Perjury is sometimes influenced by interest, and at other times by malice; but in all cases is the same God-provoking sin. Archbishop Sharp says, "In the case of other sins there may be an appeal made to God's mercy; yet in this case of perjury there is none, for he that is perjured hath precluded himself of this benefit because he hath braved God Almighty;

and hath, in effect, told him to his face that if he was foresworn he should desire no mercy."

This dreadful sin cries to heaven for vengeance from every court-house and every justice's office in the land. And then what of *official perjury*—officers of the law sworn to keep the peace and defend the law, who are among the most notorious law-breakers. Government officials, who are sworn to be faithful to their official duties, compromise their trust for the sake of gain. If there is one place in hell hotter than another these scoundrels will find that place. Among these enormous sinners may be ranked all those government officials, with those officers of the army and of the navy, who have gone into rebellion.

The crimes of profane and false swearing, which are prevalent in the country, are enough to bring down the vengeance of God upon any nation. They constitute a dismal cloud which darkens the heavens, and spreads desolation over the land. The language of the prophet Jeremiah is fearfully applicable to our own land: "For because of swearing the land mourneth; the pleasant places of the wilderness are dried up, and their course is evil, and their force is not right."

"Lying" is falsehood spoken with an intention to deceive. Dr. S. Clarke says, "The proper notion of a *lie* is an endeavoring to deceive another by signifying that to him as true which we ourselves think not to be so, in the ordinary way of communicating our thoughts." Paley says, "A *lie* is a breach of promise; for whosoever seriously addresses his discourse to another tacitly promises to speak the truth, because he knows that truth is expected." Sir Walter Raleigh says, " He which promised that he would pay money by a day, or promised anything else, whenever he faileth hath directly *lied* to him to whom the promise hath been made." Lying is a breach of one of the conditions of the social compact, and tends to the dissolution of human society. The divine rule is, "Let every man speak truth with his neighbor." Lying is stamped with the deepest criminality in the representation that " the devil is a liar, and the father of lies."

Where are the liars? They are in all ranks of society. Lies are told in business, in the common intercourse of life, in the strifes of politics. Political debates are so marked by efforts to deceive that lies in politics are hardly thought to be out of order. The great southern rebellion is sustained by stupendous lying.

"And killing." There is an awful disregard of human life in the country, independent of the demoralizing effects of the war. Murders are fearfully prevalent. Once a murder was so extraordinary an occurrence as that it convulsed the whole community; now it is so common as to be little thought of. What a tide of blood flows from the dreadful civil war now raging in this country! and how much of this is real *murder*, the day of judgment will reveal. The blood of this war will be found on somebody's skirts. Jefferson Davis says he is not responsible for it. He is fighting for the independence of the South—the North resists their claim, and must take the responsibility of all the consequences which follow. This would be legitimate enough if the independence of the South were a natural right, or if it were guaranteed by the Constitution and denied by the federal government; but neither of these things is true. Under the Constitution the southern states were as free as the northern states, and just as secure in all their rights and privileges. The rebellion is without the least provocation. It was inaugurated and is continued by wicked and ambitious leaders, on no just or honorable grounds, without the slightest necessity, and the consequence is that the guilt of all the bloodshed of the war rests upon their souls.

Saying nothing of the blood shed in battle, the cold-blooded murders, which are of every-day occurrence, reach a fearful aggregate. Hanging men upon the mere suspicion of *Abolitionism*—shooting colored prisoners, and slaughtering unarmed citizens upon pretense of their concealing their property, or refusing to take the oath of allegiance to the rebel government, or to be conscripted into their army. The aggregate of murders which have been committed in one or the other of these ways numbers thousands.

All this blood rests upon some portion of "the inhabitants of the land," and cries to heaven for vengeance. As God said to Cain, so may he say to-day to the southern chivalry, " The voice of thy brother's blood cries to me from the ground." Dr. South says, " The first great disturbance in the world, after the fall of man, was by a *murderer*, whom the vengeance of God pursued to a degree that he professed that his punishment was greater than he could bear, though he himself could not say that it was greater than he had deserved."

If murder is against the laws of humanity, what an accumulation of proof is there in the "killing " which is constantly going on, that there is a fearful deficiency of " mercy " in the land.

"Stealing." Locke says, " The taking from another what is his, without his knowledge or allowance, is properly called *stealing;* but that name being commonly understood to signify also the moral pravity of the action, and to denote its contrariety to the law, men are apt to condemn whatever they hear called stealing as an ill action, disagreeing with the rule of right." Thieving is the meanest of all callings; and yet there are many proud spirits who condescend to steal. That the business has many votaries none can doubt. At present thieves and burglars seem to be upon a rampage. No man, when he betakes himself to rest, can be certain that, when he awakes, he will not find his doors forced and his house rifled. Professional thieves—those who make stealing a business—go out from our cities in bands and penetrate the villages and the back counties. High functionaries of the government *steal* from the public purse. This is so *genteel* a method of getting money that it is scarcely thought to be either wicked or mean. If an officer takes any amount from the government, be it great or small, without authority, and not rendering a fair account of the same, he commits a *theft:* and those who commit theft, from the petty thefts of the servant-girl to that of the notorious Governor Floyd, are *thieves*, and are to be ranked with other classes of abominable sinners.

"And committing adultery." The sin here named is one of the crying sins of these times. The sin itself and its connections—what leads to it and what follows it—permeate the very texture of society. These are vulgar vices, but they are by no means confined to what is called vulgar society. They exist to an alarming extent among the higher classes—in educated and fashionable society. We have not yet reached the depth of licentiousness which sapped the foundations of the Roman empire, and brought about the French Revolution, yet we are taking fearful strides in the same direction. How many wrecks, scattered all along the coast, warn us of its perils. Broken family circles and bleeding hearts testify of the fearful prevalence of the mischief.

What shall I say further? I must not say too

much, for by so doing I might help on the evil which I would fain remedy. This crime is one of the most corrupting of all the vices. It strikes in all directions. It is a sin against God, against human society, and against one's self. It shows at once the absence of "truth," of "mercy," and "the knowledge of God." Where it prevails—and God knows it does almost everywhere—it marks the decay of all the virtues.

The fearful prevalence of the aforesaid crimes is indicated in the expression, " they break out." They are seen in terrible *outbreaks*. As a smoldering fire breaks out of a building; as the burning lava breaks out from a volcano, sending down the mountain sides torrents of fire, overwhelming towns and cities, and desolating fertile plains, one outbreak follows another until all animal life and every green thing are destroyed.

"And blood touches blood." The blood of one slain victim reaches to that of another, and the whole surface of the ground is covered with gore. What a figure is this! and yet scarcely a figure. The land is deluged with the blood of the slain, and yet the work of death goes on. Millions cry, "O earth, cover not thou our blood, and let our cry come forth!"

Now what is the condition of the public mind in view of all this awful weight of criminality? I fear that as a nation we are not penitent. To-day we are indulging in pride and extravagant outlays, just as if several hundred thousands of our sons and brothers had not been swept away. Our people are swinging out in pleasure in all forms, some of them new, while the pall of death covers the face of the whole country. The voice of weeping which is heard in every town and neighborhood is overborne by the noise of music and dancing.

We have had our days of fasting and prayer; but have they been characterized by that evidence of deep and hearty contrition which they should have been? Our fasts have not been much like that of Nineveh. Nor have they in all cases been productive of the fruits described by the holy prophet. Isaiah lviii, 3, 5, 6.

The controversy, and the method by which it is prosecuted.

The present gigantic civil war is one of the means which God in his providence sees proper to employ for the punishment of the nation for her sins.

The southern people have grievously offended, in their cruel oppression of the African race, and in inaugurating this war. These things they have done in addition to having a full share in the corruptions of which I have before spoken, and they are greater sufferers from the consequences of the war than the people of the North. Let the hundreds of thousands of their slain, and their desolated fields, bear testimony to the fury of the storm which they have invoked. The war is working as a punishment of a most fearful character for their terrible crimes; yet as we of the North are guilty of many and aggravated offenses, we are awfully punished. As God often uses one wicked people for the punishment of another, he is permitting this slaveholders' rebellion to inflict upon us terrible chastisement. How many Rachels are mourning for their children, refusing to be comforted because they are not? How many widowed wives and orphan children are left in loneliness and helplessness in every portion of the country? This war lays an awful tribute upon the population of the free North, and the curse has not come causeless.

The explanation is what I have before premised, that God often uses one wicked people for the punishment of another. He employed the wicked Assyrian king for the punishment of his own people, while that king was at the same time moved by ambition, and treasuring up a fearful harvest of divine wrath. The case is thus announced by the prophet: "O Assyrian, the rod of mine anger, and the staff in their hand is mine indignation. I will send him against a hypocritical nation, and against the people of my wrath will I give him a charge, to take the spoil, and to take the prey, and to tread them down like the mire of the streets. Howbeit he meaneth not so, neither doth his heart think so; but it is in his heart to destroy and cut off nations not a few."

Our southern enemies have no intention of fulfilling

the councils of heaven in chastising us for our sins, in which they themselves have had a prominent part; but their object is to destroy the unity of the nation, and to build up an independent nationality *resting upon slavery as its chief corner-stone.* Their ambitious and diabolical project shall utterly fail, but in the mean time they have inflicted upon us fearful punishment.

God has allowed us to suffer reverses, and by their means suffers the war to be protracted.

This fact is no favor to the rebels, nor any indication of the final failure of our cause. The problems of Providence are often slow of solution. We needed humbling, and may be we need it still, and God may see still further occasion to try us. And if I read Providence aright this war is to be the means, in the hands of Providence, of making an end of slavery, and the extent and continuance of it are to be used, in the divine economy, for this end. If the war had lasted but a year the institution would have survived, and the same elements of discord which have troubled the country from the beginning of its history would have remained. With every year of its continuance *the peculiar institution* has been losing its vitality, until it is in its dying agonies. The continuance of the war is a scourge to the North, but it is breaking down the slave power of the South. It is a severe discipline to us, and a judicial punishment to the southern slaveholders; while it is a furnace to melt off the chains of four million of slaves, and thus to restore them to the rights of men. How much longer God will contend with us he only knows. We pray that the work may be cut short in righteousness.

The guilty South will finally fall.

We have seen that God used the Assyrian king to punish the disobedience of the Jews; but what did he do with that king at last? (See Isaiah x, 8, 13–19, 24–27.)

The overshadowing Assyrian power, when the time of divine visitation had come, was dashed to pieces like a potter's vessel, and never recovered. Vitringa remarks that "all the characters of this prophecy belong to Sennacherib, though possibly it may have a more extensive scope, and refer to the destruction of all the enemies of God, and the following great empires which God made use of as rods and scourges to chastise and amend his people." Bishop Newton observes that "as the Assyrians totally destroyed the kingdom of Israel, and greatly oppressed that of Judah, no wonder they are the subject of several prophecies. The prophet here denounceth the judgments of God against Sennacherib in particular, and against the Assyrians in general. God might employ them as ministers of his wrath, and executioners of his vengeance, and so make the wickedness of some nations the means of correcting that of others."

The illustration is complete. When God had done using Sennacherib as an instrument, he destroyed both him and his army. Some confidently believe that when he has done using the southern slave oligarchy as a scourge, he will then destroy it. This great "controversy" will terminate in the hopeless and irretrievable ruin of the political power of Jefferson Davis, and the utter annihilation of all his fancies of a great slave empire in "the sunny South." His schemes and his despotism will tumble into ruin together, and "none will be so poor as to do him reverence." May the God of the Universe hasten it in his time! *Amen.*

VIII.

THE WRATH OF MAN SHALL PRAISE GOD.

SURELY THE WRATH OF MAN SHALL PRAISE THEE: THE REMAINDER OF WRATH SHALT THOU RESTRAIN.—Psa. lxxvi, 10.

PROVIDENCE has great problems which time sometimes solves. It is difficult for us to see how that which is evil and only evil can be followed by beneficent results. Leaving God out of the question, we can think of no rule of judgment except that which declares that "an evil tree cannot bring forth good fruit;" we therefore estimate the result by the character of the cause. The doctrine of a universal and particular providence will effectually guard against the hasty conclusion that any event, however evil in itself, or mischievous in its immediate results, may not be overruled for good. "The wrath of man worketh not the righteousness of God," and yet God can so work by his providence that the wrath of man may be made to go out of its natural course and subserve the righteousness of God. "Surely the wrath of man shall praise thee."

In the discussion of this subject I propose

To explain the doctrine that the wrath of man shall praise God.

The Hebrew word חֵמָה, *hamat*, wrath, is from a root which signifies *heat*, or to become *warm*, and is figuratively applied to *anger*, *lust*, or any unholy excitement in men. The text may consequently be applied to anger, malice, envy, ambition, covetousness, or lust. We here have a large class of the evil principles and impulses which inhabit the human heart, and break out into forms of sin or crime against the laws of God or of society; and all these are subject to the laws of the divine government asserted in the text, which I make the foundation of the present discourse. All the malignant passions of the depraved human heart are so overruled as to be made subservient to the cause of truth and righteousness.

Malice and envy are the passions of devils, but they are found in luxuriant growth in the human bosom. The evidence of them is cruel injustice and oppression, wrong and misery inflicted upon others, with evil intent.

> Men that make
> Envy and crooked malice nourishment,
> Do bite the best.—SHAKSPEARE.

The ambitious man seeks his own glory at any cost. If others stand in his way he pulls them down. They may be much better than himself, but, as though he had a divine right to the coveted position, he demands that they succumb and allow him to rise upon their ruins.

> I charge thee, fling away ambition;
> By that sin fell the angels: how can man, then,
> The image of his Maker, hope to win by't?
> Love thyself least, cherish those hearts that hate thee;
> Corruption wins not more than honesty.
> Still in thy right hand carry gentle peace,
> To silence envious tongues. Be just and fear not;
> Let all the ends thou aim'st at be thy country's,
> Thy God's and truth's.—SHAKSPEARE.

Ambition is insatiable. It storms the giddiest height, and yet looks higher; it feeds on empty air and hopes to be filled, but is still empty; it grasps everything, and loses all.

> Ambition, when the pinnacle is gained
> With many a toilsome step, the power it sought
> Wants to support itself, and sighs to find
> The envied height, but aggravates the fall.
>   GEORGE BALLY.

Covetousness incontinently desires the wealth of the world. It ever demands more. Like the two daughters of the horse-leech, it cries, "Give, give!"

> O cursed lust of gold, when for thy sake
> The fool throws up his interest in both worlds;
> First starved in this, then damned in that to come.—BLAIR.

The baser passions, when unrestrained, carry their victim down the stream of indulgence to the stagnant pool of dissipation. The excessive indulgence of the animal passions sinks the rational into the animal nature; the image of God is degraded into mere brutality, and the immortal nature receives the impression of the beast.

> Earthly desires and sensual lust
> Are passions springing from the dust;
> They fade and die;

> But in the life beyond the tomb
> They seal the immortal spirit's doom
> Eternally.—MANRIQUE.

The vile principles and passions of men shall be made to praise God. The outbreaking of human corruption is intended to injure an individual or society generally, but it is made to praise God. The malicious and envious may plot mischief, but their schemes are overturned, and God is glorified. Villains may contrive to circumvent the unwary and enrich themselves, or gratify their evil passions; but God confounds them, and makes them unwilling instruments of his pleasure.

God sets limits to human passions.

"The remainder of wrath shalt thou restrain."

The evil dispositions of men will not be allowed to go beyond what God will make to praise him. When human passions have reached the bounds of divine permission God says: "Hitherto shalt thou come and no further, and here shall thy proud waves be stayed." What is permitted will be overruled for good, and all that remains shall be restrained. No more wrath than will be turned to God's account will he allow. How far human passions would proceed if it were not for God's restraining providence, we may not be able to determine; but thus much we may know, to wit, that whatever occurs is subject to the divine control, and is made to serve some valuable purpose. What remains, if it were not restrained, would lay waste the fair heritage of God. It is to be attributed to divine restraint that wickedness has not secured the mastery and blasted forever every bud of promise in the moral world. The good there is here exists in spite of evil, and not by its kind indulgence.

The designs of wicked men are turned aside even when they are permitted to accomplish their evil schemes. They execute their evil schemes when the ends which they propose to accomplish are wholly disappointed. They have an end in view in their calculations, and God has another in the plans of his providence, and their objects and aims are thwarted and the ends of divine wisdom are consummated. When a wicked project begins to succeed it is a great error to conclude that it will succeed in the end, or that the wicked devices of the perverted intellect engaged in it will finally succeed. There are many ways in which Providence can frustrate the whole scheme, even down to the very point of success.

The effects of a wicked device may be wholly turned aside. The poisoned arrow may miss its object and fall harmlessly on the ground. God is a shield to the righteous, and no weapon formed against them shall prosper. So far as the cause of God and the interests of the Church are concerned they are safe in the divine keeping whatever instrumentality may be employed against them.

Persecution has often been employed for the suppression or ruin of a good cause, but has generally proved a failure. It has indeed made martyrs, but every martyr it has made has not been an instance of defeat. An old father says, " The blood of the martyrs is the seed of the Church." It is one thing to silence the voice of a reformer, and another to crush a reformation. One set of agents employed in the support of a cause may be disposed of, but God can raise up another, or, if need be, can sustain the cause without agents. "There is no wisdom nor understanding nor counsel against the Lord."

Infidelity has had its malicious plots against the Church, and has laid science and learning under contribution for the destruction of her strong foundations, but its best laid schemes have failed of their desired results. Organizations have been formed, lectures founded, and books written against the claims of divine revelation, but they have only had the effect to call forth the talents of the Church in its defense, and of adding new triumphs of the cause of revealed religion. Paine's "Age of Reason" has malice enough in it to annihilate Christianity, and to curse the whole world; but it may well be doubted whether it has had the least effect to impede the progress of the Gospel in the world. God takes care that the natural consequences of every assault made upon the truth of Christianity shall be turned aside; and that, in spite of the malice of men and devils, the kingdom of Christ shall march steadily on to the consummation of his grand and glorious purposes.

I shall finally proceed to give some illustrations of the doctrine of the text.

Illustrations are scattered so abundantly through the pages of the Bible and of profane history that it is difficult to select. A few only among the many can be employed.

For the first instance I take the oppression and persecution of the children of Israel in Egypt.

Pharaoh's object was to prevent the too great increase and growth of the Israelites, and to discipline them to slavery. The terrible oppressions to which the people of Israel were subjected were not allowed by Providence to proceed so far as to annihilate, or even to diminish them. Indeed, "the more they afflicted them the more they multiplied and grew." When the people had escaped from Egypt, Pharaoh pursued them with his army and hemmed them in at the Red Sea; but there he was destroyed.

As a part of the system of God's restraining providence should be taken into the account the plagues with which Egypt was visited and Pharaoh's infidelity was rebuked. The Lord said to Pharaoh, "And in very deed for this cause have I raised thee up, for to show in thee my power; and that my name may be declared throughout all the earth." Pharaoh's design was to hold the children of Israel in bondage, and make their enslavement a source of great gain; but he reached a point where his way was hedged up, and he became the unwilling instrument of a glorious manifestation of divine power and providence. He kicked against the restraint until he fell before it. If this great offender had ceased from his furor of rebellion early in his conflict with God, he might have escaped the terrible catastrophe which befell him; but he poured out his wrath to the bitter end, and it was made to praise God. Here is a fearful example of the fact that when a man is so saturated with wrath that no indications of the divine judgments will bring him to terms, summary destruction is at hand.

The next illustration I give is the case of *Joseph*.

There are two instances in the history of Joseph which illustrate the doctrine of the text. The first is his being sold into Egypt by his brethren. The ruling principle which moved the brethren of Joseph to sell him was *envy*. Joseph was his father's favorite, and acted as a sort of spy to report to his father the misdeeds of his brethren. His prophetic dreams, which foreshadow his elevation above his brethren, were matters of serious offense and jealousy. Availing themselves of a favorable occasion, they sold him to a caravan of Ishmaelitish merchants, and contrived a scheme to make their father believe that he had been devoured by a wild beast. The brothers intended to remove Joseph from the family circle, and thereafter to be rid of his watchful and reproving eye. There was a mixture of bad passions developed in this transaction. There was added to envy, malice, wounded pride, jealousy, and some of the meanness of cupidity. They sold him for twenty pieces of silver, about three pounds sterling, or half the price of a slave on the African coast in modern times. Now they supposed Joseph fairly out of their way.

The consequences of this flagrant instance of wickedness were taken under the guidance of Providence, and, after several strange changes and threatening reverses, Joseph became governor of Egypt and the deliverer of his family from death by famine. When Joseph made himself known to his brethren he gave them his construction of the theology taught in the whole matter of his coming to Egypt. "Now therefore," he says, "be not grieved, nor angry with yourselves, that ye sold me hither: for God did send me before you to preserve life." " Surely the wrath of man shall praise thee, and the remainder of wrath shalt thou restrain." The illustration is perfect. Their wickedness was arrested at the precise point where it was not to be made a further instrument of showing forth the glory of God.

Another instance in the history of Joseph, in which a vile passion was made to praise God, was the wicked passion and the base falsehood of the wife of Potiphar. A disappointed wicked woman stops at nothing. In this case, to conceal her own shame, she falsely accuses Joseph, and, to all human appearance, effects his utter ruin. He is cast into a vile prison among presumed felons. There God prepared a train of circumstances which led to his elevation to the position of a prince in the kingdom. What human wisdom could have turned such malign dispositions and schemes to such glorious account? That wicked woman thought to deprive Joseph of all power as an informer or a witness; but God used her wicked schemes to invest him with the dignity of a prophet, the power of a great civil ruler, and a benefactor of the Egyptians and of his father's house.

The story of Joseph has the charm of a beautiful and skillfully constructed romance. The hero of the tale is a splendid character; indeed, everything that could be desired. His story is full of marvels, and it ascends to the dizzy heights of power and influence without being marred by a single vice or weakness. A more wonderful character and a greater moral hero than Joseph is not found in the history of man; and what is remarkable is that the great facts in his story are illustrations and confirmations of the doctrine that God uses the vilest instruments and the vilest acts for the manifestation of his own glory.

Passing a multitude of historical facts and events which might advantageously be seized upon as illustrations of my theme, I select the persecutions of the Puritans.

The uncompromising war which commenced on "popish rags" and English formalism, by an earnest stern class of the descendants of the Reformation, resulted in a relentless persecution. After the Reformation from popery in England, the English sovereigns continued to administer the government upon the principle of uniformity, claiming the right to force the consciences of the worshipers into conformity with the forms and usages of the national establishment. The Puritans demanded liberty of conscience; the government denied this right; and the consequence was that great numbers of godly pastors were ejected from their parishes, and their hungry flocks were deprived of their pastoral oversight.

The relentless persecutions which followed, with fines and imprisonment, under the Stuarts, sent away to the wilds of America both pastors and flocks in great numbers. The New England colonies were principally peopled with refugees, who loved liberty of conscience more than the quiet possession of home and plenty, and sought that precious boon in the western wilderness. They chose liberty among the wild beasts and merciless savages rather than to be restrained in the free exercise of their consciences in honor and abundance. God smiled upon the fugitive colonists, and the wilderness soon budded and blossomed as the rose. The result has been a successful experiment in the way of a free government, and a Church untrammeled by the State.

The Act of Uniformity under the reign of Charles II., and the persecution which followed, were designed to stifle dissent, and to settle the question of the right of the state to establish a uniform system of religious worship. In the mind of God, however, this unscriptural and unphilosophical system of compulsion, in matters of conscience, was to be judged and condemned by an experiment which it forced on by its struggles for ascendency. Persecution which was designed to annihilate dissent, organized and established its fundamental principles and forms upon the western continent, and sent over Europe a tide of light in favor of "a State without a king and a Church without a bishop." The whole history of the American Church has been a standing reproof of the system of constrained obedience to forms and ceremonies of man's devising. The great principle of a free Gospel, a free Church, and a free conscience, may now be considered as settled forever.

The fourth and last illustration which I shall present of the doctrine of the text is the great slaveholders' rebellion, with which the nation is at present contending.

It may be considered hazardous to use unfinished history to illustrate a principle. The rebellion not yet being completed, it may be supposed impossible to say whether it will be an instance of successful rebellion or an utter failure. The progress of the conflict thus far, and the indications of what will probably occur at no distant date, afford data for a tolerably correct conclusion with regard to the class of instructive historical events with which the great American rebellion is finally to be associated. Coming events cast their shadows before them. The dispatches of these few days past unmistakably indicate that the time for writing the history of the rebellion has nearly arrived.* At all events I shall venture to assume what will be the character of the lesson which that history will teach.

Several theories, in turn, have been promulgated by the rebel savans of the objects of the rebellion. One is, that it is resistance of northern aggression; another, that it is in defense of their domestic institutions; and another, that it is to establish southern independence. Whichever of these be the cause which has originated the movement, or whether all have had a hand in it, is not material, so far as the investigation in hand is concerned. In either case the rebellion originated in false or vicious principles. It is the offshoot of pride, ambition, lust of power, or a love of human bondage, or all together. The aggressions which they speak of are imaginary; the slavery which they would protect and perpetuate is a system of injustice; and as for southern independence, it is not a right of the southern people. The rebellion is based upon false assumptions, and is carried on by a system of plunder and wholesale murder.

* Written December 16, 1864.

Now the question is, How God is managing the results of this deluge of wrath which the southern slaveholders are pouring out? If I understand the movements of Providence, the rebellion is working out the destruction of slavery and the humiliation of the slave oligarchy. These results are evidently in the mind of God in the whole process. The rebel leaders meant to create a government with slavery for its chief corner-stone, and to establish an order of nobility—an upper grade of society. God is working for the disappointment of these projects—the destruction of the system of slavery, and the humiliation and overthrow of the southern aristocracy. When the rebellion shall have gone as far as God sees good for the accomplishment of these designs, it will be restrained.

War in itself is a terrible scourge and an awful calamity. It is almost always the product of wicked passions. Its evils are innumerable. It is a yawning gulf, which swallows up millions of treasure and millions of precious lives without being satisfied. It will be a difficult problem to solve what is the amount of destruction which the war of the rebellion has occasioned. The judgment-day alone will bring to light the terrible guilt of this war. We may apply to the authors of it, with some little variations, the prophetic curse which the patriarch Jacob pronounced upon Simeon and Levi: "Instruments of cruelty are in their habitations. O my soul, come not thou into their secret; unto their assembly, mine honor, be not thou united: for in their anger they slew a man, and in their self-will they digged down a wall. Cursed be their anger, for it was fierce; and their wrath, for it was cruel: I will divide them in Jacob, and scatter them in Israel." Gen. xlix, 5-7.

Fearful as this war is in its destruction of life and property, it will undoubtedly be overruled for the good of the world. God has his own method in dealing with it. It is a fact which history abundantly establishes, that great national reforms are preceded by a baptism of blood. Sometimes there are evils in the body politic which the peaceful measures of progress are not suited to remove—they can only be purged out by fire and the sword. Wicked men and corrupt principles must be removed. War is waged upon the peace and the rights of society, and the ambitious and wicked agents engaged in it, under the control of Providence, destroy themselves, they and their refuges of lies perishing together. God knows how to manage the ship of state in a great national tempest. He knows when to suffer the wrath of designing and wicked men to proceed and when to restrain it. When he has no further use for the present civil war he will bring it to an end. He will make it contribute largely to the advancement of the race in knowledge and virtue. His kingdom shall be advanced, and made to triumph by ".the wrath of man."

I shall close this discourse with a few observations. The wrath of man is not occasioned or brought about by God. The wrath is man's work, man's sin. The overruling it is entirely distinct from the thing itself. The guilt and responsibility of the wrong is with the transgressor, but it is God's part to see that it does not accomplish the destructive ends which it designs: more, he will make it minister to the praise of his glorious name.

The guilty originator of an evil scheme is just as culpable as he would be if it had accomplished all the mischief which was intended. That the flood of wrath which is poured out by wicked men and devils does not affect all the ruin intended is no credit to them. They are just as responsible and as guilty when it is all made to praise God, as they would have been if it had desolated the land, and blasted every bud of hope for the future of the Church and the world.

Although God uses wicked men for the accomplishment of his grand designs, he is not therefore dependent upon them. If men should cease to pour out their wrath, it is not to be supposed God's resources would fail. His praise would still be sounded out through the vast universe by innumerable voices. Heaven above and the earth beneath would be full of harmony. The starry heavens would declare the glory of God, and the firmament would show forth his handiwork. If the wrath of man is made to praise God, his love and obedience would contribute much more to the measure of glory to which he is entitled. That Divine Providence uses the evil agencies of earth and hell for purposes of good, is an exhibition of the wealth and not of the poverty of the divine resources. He who can glorify himself through the very wrath of his enemies must be infinite in resources.

We may rejoice to know that a time is coming when there will be no more "wrath of man," but love and the feelings of a common brotherhood shall be universal. The day is not far distant when men shall "beat their swords into plowshares and their spears into pruning-hooks;" when the baser passions shall be purged out from the earth, and the heavenly principles of charity and mutual good-will shall grace the various grades of society, sanctify the family, give character to the intercourse of nations, and crown the Church with millennial glory.

IX.

SLAVERY.

AND HORSES, AND CHARIOTS, AND SLAVES, AND SOULS OF MEN.
Rev. xviii, 13.

The word σωματων, rendered *slaves*, should be *bodies: bodies and souls of men*. A parallel passage is to be found in Ezek. xxvii, 13: "They traded the persons of men and vessels of brass in thy market." The word *persons* does not give the specific idea of the original, בְּנֶפֶשׁ אָדָם, *in souls of men*. Sept., *Souls of men*. The bodies and souls of men were matters of commerce in Tyre and in Rome; that is, they traded in *slaves* the same as they did in "vessels of brass," in "chariots," and in "horses." The bodies and souls of men were mixed up with beasts of burden and all sorts of material commodities. This is precisely the idea of southern slavery under the laws of the slave states. Slaves in these laws are defined "*chattels personal, to all intents and purposes.*"

The exigencies of the controversy on the subject of slavery have called forth a variety of definitions of the institution. A learned doctor, who has written a book upon the subject, defines slavery *service*. A wife owes to her husband *service*, a child owes his parents *service*, and if it is a moral wrong for a master to enforce service upon a slave, that gentleman demands, is it not morally wrong to require service of a wife or a son? This is a palpable and a senseless sophism. This definition of slavery is no definition at all. A definition is a statement of the genus and the difference. We have the genus here, but have not the species, or the difference between slavery and any other species of service. Saying that slavery is service is saying nothing. We want to know the conditions of the service, on what ground the master claims it, how he enforces it, how long it continues, and what effect it has upon the posterity of the slave. Clearly, if the service of a wife and of a son does not imply the right of property, and consequently the right of sale, we cannot reason from one to the other. One may be consistent with the laws of humanity and justice while the other is not. What then is slavery? What is African slavery in the slave states of the South? This is the question which I shall attempt to answer.

What is African slavery in the slave states of America?

I do not now discuss Hebrew bondage nor the slavery of the ancients, but the slavery of the African race as it exists in this country.

This species of slavery implies complete ownership.

The slave is the property of his master, subject to all the conditions of any other species of property. He is absolutely subject to the will of his master, liable to sale as much as a horse or an ox, and consequently liable to be separated from all his home associations and relations. The wife is separated from the husband, and the husband from the wife; the child from the parent, and the parent from the child. The slave descends to heirs-at-law the same as any other property, and is sold at sheriff's sale for debt the same as oxen or horses. The slave is not regarded by the slave code as a *person*, but as a thing, a mere article of trade.

The slave's *body* and *soul* are sold in the market. Strength and agility, health and comeliness, all go to enhance the value of the slave, and these properties are sold. Intellectual and moral qualities are taken into the account in the sale of a slave. If the slave has genius, that genius is sold; if he has mechanical skill, that skill is sold; if he has moral qualities they are sold; if he has a conscience, that conscience is sold; if he is a Christian, his religion is sold; if he is a Methodist exhorter, or a Baptist preacher, his gifts are sold. His soul goes with his body to the auction block. The grace and the image of God and the purchase of the Saviour's blood go under the hammer like the qualities of a blood-hound or an old wagon. Slave dealers "trade in the bodies and the souls of men." It is essential to *a man* that he own himself; it is essential to a woman that she have control over her own person; but the slave is wholly the property of another, and, so far as it is possible, is subject to his control, body and soul. Slavery consequently denudes the slave of all that constitutes him an intelligent, moral, and responsible being. The slave may think in spite of his master, but so far as thought comes out in actions he can only think in one way. He may love God, but his religious affections must be subordinated to the will of his owner.

In a limited sense it must be admitted that a slave may be a Christian; but it is only in such a sense as, under compulsion, religion can survive a violation of the moral law. When this can take place I leave for the Judge of all the earth to determine.

Under these conditions the responsibilities of a slaveholder are fearful beyond all conception. He is responsible for the actions, the life, the character, and the eternal destiny of his slaves. If slaves are compelled to minister to the brutal passions of their masters, and by that means are eternally lost, what a weight of responsibility rests upon the shoulders of the master. They are guilty of the blood of the victims of their lust. An awful weight of responsibility rests upon their souls which they will have to meet before the bar of God. Slaveholding in the mildest form involves too great a responsibility for any human being, and by a good conscience should be shunned as the gates of hell.

The slave is held for life. The Jewish servant was set free from servitude on the year of release, but the slave of the South is held absolutely at the pleasure of his master; and more recently the laws of the slave states prohibit emancipation, or surround it with so many difficulties that it amounts to a legal impossibility for the slaveholder to give freedom to his slaves. Death only releases the poor African slave from his inexorable doom.

One of the conditions of slavery is that the descendants of the slave, to the latest generation, are slaves. Under the divine law " the son shall not bear the iniquity of the father." Why should the son be a slave because his *mother* was a slave? If all men are created free, as we have a right to assume that they are, and as that immortal bill of rights, the Declaration of American Independence, asserts, no human being can be born a slave. The idea of hereditary slavery is only suitable to the barbarous ages. The idea of individuality and individual responsibility, which is so clearly maintained in this advanced period of the world's history, is utterly at war with that essential feature of African slavery which entails servitude upon the descendants of the slave forever. Bad enough, too bad, that the slave should have no hope of personal liberty during his natural life, but overwhelmingly horrible that his offspring should be doomed to the same condition of vassalage to the latest generation.

I shall next proceed to give a sketch of the history of slavery.

Slavery had its origin in the barbarous ages. Clans and nations of savages made war upon each other, and made slaves of those who were taken captives. The patriarchs held servants, but although they were sometimes purchased they were not sold, but often became heir to their master's estate. They were the stewards of the house, and often transacted all the outdoor business. "Eliezer of Damascus" was Abram's servant, and before Isaac was born was his "heir." It is universally held by commentators that it was this same Eliezer with whom was intrusted the important business of negotiating for a wife for Isaac. Servitude under the patriarchs was tempered with justice, confidence, and forbearance, and it must have been a blessing to slaves among the heathen to be purchased into comparative freedom. There was little of the elements of the cruel heathen bondage, or of African slavery, in the servitude which was in use among the patriarchs.

The Jews held the heathen in slavery under a temporary divine sanction. The ancient Greeks reduced a caste to slavery. The Helots were bought and sold as slaves, and were in a condition of abject bondage. The Romans and the ancient Germans held slaves. Captives taken in war from nearly all the nations of the world were sold in Rome like beasts in the shambles. These slaves were generally white, and not inferior to their conquerors in intelligence and civilization. In the sixth century Pope Gregory saw Englishmen in the slave-market in Rome who were of so fair a countenance, and so fine an appearance generally, that he said, "call them not *Angli* but *Angeli.*" Considering it a pity that such a race should be without the Gospel, the Pope sent the monk Augustine to England to convert the people to Rome. This piece of history is referred to in proof that slaves were not anciently selected from inferior races.

Negro slavery sprung up much later than the times of which I have yet spoken. In the wars between Carthage and Rome, Romans and Carthagenians were alternately made slaves. There was no enslavement of color or of caste. The same was the fact from the period of the highest glory of the Roman empire to its decline and fall. African slaves came into request in later times.

The African slave-trade had its origin after the discovery of America, to supply the West Indies with laborers. The Portuguese were the first to engage in the murderous work of stealing the poor negroes from their quiet bowers, selling them into perpetual bondage. The Dutch navigators brought the first African slaves to North America. In 1551 the English began to trade in negroes, and in 1556 Sir John Hawkins sailed with two ships to

Cape Verde, whence he sent out men to capture negroes. The following order to the colonial government at New York from Queen Anne is remarkable. They were to "take care that the Almighty should be devoutly and duly served according to the rites of the Church of England, and also that the Royal African Company should be encouraged, and that the colony should have a constant and sufficient supply of *merchantable* negroes at moderate rates." The British government had this nefarious trade under its supervision until it was abolished in 1807.

The hand which the parent government had in bringing to her colonies such a vast mass of slaves is made matter of complaint in Jefferson's original draft of the Declaration of Independence. It was a great branch of commerce which kept the English vessels in profitable employment. Our statesmen, at the formation of the federal Constitution, did not allow the word *slave* or *slavery* to be incorporated into that instrument, supposing that the institution would gradually die out. The exigences of the cotton-growing business, however, created a demand for labor in the southern states, and African slavery came to be considered a necessity. An "irrepressible conflict" between slave and free labor sprung up, and has been in progress until the opening of the existing rebellion. During the last thirty years especially the question of slavery has been discussed in the country politically, economically, and morally, until the subject ought to be well understood by all thoughtful people.

A multitude of books have been written upon the various aspects of the subject of slavery. Its history and bearings have been copiously delineated, and the literature of the subject can scarcely be mastered by a person of ordinary capacity in a lifetime. I must content myself with having given a mere sketch.*

I shall next notice the principal arguments by which slavery is defended.

It was once quite a popular argument, or at least an assumed reason in favor of African slavery, that the African race is doomed to perpetual slavery by the irrevocable decree of heaven. The proof of this proposition is found in the prophetic curse of Noah: "Cursed be Canaan; a servant of servants shall he be to his brethren." Gen. ix, 25.

In order to make out an argument from this text two assumptions are made. The *first* is, that the descendants of Canaan were *black;* and *secondly*, that the curse in the case dooms them all to slavery.

In answer to the first assumption, let it be observed that the Canaanites were not negroes. The denial of this assumption is sufficient until proof is offered; but it may here be noted that Canaan settled on the

---

* An excellent sketch of the history of slavery may be found in Appleton's American Encyclopedia, article, Slavery.

east of the Mediterranean in Asia, while the negro race is universally admitted to have been first found in Africa.

As to the second assumption, that Noah pronounces the doom of perpetual slavery upon the descendants of Canaan, it may be observed that nothing more is necessarily to be understood by this curse than that the Canaanites should be a conquered people, as in fact they were under Joshua. Having been subdued in the land of Canaan, the nations which descended from Ham either remained in a state of vassalage in the land of promise, or were scattered among other nations. Calmet tells us that the remnants of these conquered nations fled to Greece and Egypt, and ultimately were settled in many portions of Asia and Africa.

If we admit that Noah's curse is meant for the descendants of Canaan, and they are the negroes, what is the logical consequence? It implies that the negroes are servants to their "brethren." Are the southern slaveholders "*brethren*" to the slaves? Southern slaveholders generally consider their slaves an inferior race, scarcely human. They would consider it an insult to be told that they hold their "brethren" in slavery. Their sympathizers at the North do not hold that "the niggers" are *brothers* to their *masters*, and yet they use this "cursed-be-Canaan" argument as though it made an end of the controversy. Let slaveholders have the argument for all it is worth if they will, but we will hold them to the concession which their employment of it necessarily implies—that they hold their "*brethren*" in *cruel bondage*. In whatever light this famous passage is viewed, it contains no warrant for negro slavery.

It is often asserted that the natural condition of the negro is that of slavery. He is ignorant and degraded, incapable of self-government, and the like. If ignorance and degradation, and a consequent inability for self-government, are reasons which justify the enslavement of one people, why do not the same reasons justify the reduction to slavery of all other people who are in the same condition? A strong people has no more right to enslave a weak people than a strong individual has a right to exact the sweat and toil of him who is weaker because he may be able to enforce it. Slavery is not the natural condition of any human being. No one loses his rights because he is weak or ignorant. The weak and the ignorant are entitled to charity instead of oppression at the hands of those who are their superiors in strength and wisdom.

Jewish servitude is employed to prove the right of slavery.

The law of servitude is found in the twenty-fifth chapter of Leviticus. There is a distinction made in the law between the Israelite and the stranger. The Israelite was not to be ruled over "with rigor," and he should have his freedom at the end of six years, or in "the year of jubilee." There is nothing in this temporary and qualified servitude analogous to negro slavery. This will be admitted. It is, however, contended that the Israelites were authorized to hold in perpetual slavery "the children of the strangers"— "the heathen," or the Gentile nations.

Let it be observed that this arrangement does not subject one heathen nation any more than another to the condition of slavery, much less does it say anything about the African race; and who will say that all who are not Jews are by this law subjected to the conditions of slavery?

No authority is here given to *sell* a slave. Without the right to sell, slavery loses a large portion of its horrors. The separation of husbands and wives, of parents and children, which is so common an incident in the slave states, would never occur after the owner had come into possession of a slave under the law.

This law does not entail slavery upon the children of the slave. This, it may be plead, is a matter of course, and is to be presumed. It is not a matter of course. The law cannot be made to embrace anything which it does not express, and it says nothing about the condition of slavery descending to the posterity of the slave.

The servitude authorized in the law in question cannot be regarded as of permanent and universal obligation. Like the Jewish law of divorce, it was temporary and local. It is applicable to no other people, and has long since been disused among the Jews themselves. Concubinage was once allowed, but is now condemned by all Christian people.

Again, the law distinctly recognizes the right of a slave to leave his master. There was not only an entire omission of law for the reclamation of fugitive slaves, but there was a direct statute for the protection of the fugitive. "Thou shalt not deliver unto his master the servant which is escaped from his master unto thee: he shall dwell with thee. . . . Thou shalt not oppress him." Deut. xxiii, 15, 16.

It is asserted that slavery is recognized and regulated by Christ and his apostles, and consequently we are to consider the institution as sanctioned in the teachings of the New Testament.

Let it be observed that the condition of slavery was sanctioned by the Roman law, and was one of the usages of civil society in the apostolic age. As it was no part of the Saviour's mission to revolutionize governments, or to interfere with man's social relations, he did not command the Christian master to give civil liberty to his slaves, but required him so to modify his treatment of them that they would be slaves but in name. That great law, "As ye would that men should do unto you do ye even so to them," is of universal obligation, and if practiced by the master would give the slave his liberty, at least in fact, if not in form.

St. Paul applies this principle to the treatment of slaves. He says: "Masters, give unto your servants that which is just and equal; knowing that ye also have a Master in heaven." Col. iv, 1. Whatever glosses may have been put upon this passage, I am not able to avoid the conclusion that the apostle meant by "just and equal" *an equivalent for their services.* What is just and equal in one case is just and equal in another. Some of the commentators seem to think that the apostle refers to food, clothing, and physic — what the Roman law allowed a slave. To me it seems obvious that he meant more. It seems to bring down to nothing the scope of a grave Christian precept to make it mean mere *heathen honesty.* The mind of the apostle certainly contemplated a higher rule of duty than that which Roman society recognized, embracing the new relations of the parties established by the new Christian life. The addition of the word *equal* after *just* gives double force to the duty required, and would seem to forbid the idea that all that is intended is a mere coming up to the standard established by the custom of the country. The apostle rather recognizes a common meed of justice and equity which applies to all, and consists in an application of our Saviour's golden rule. If the man converted to Christianity finds himself a master in possession of slaves, he is thenceforth to treat the persons who, in law, hold the relation of slaves to him with the justice to which *men* are entitled, and this done, their bondage is merely nominal.

There is another precept which the apostle gives to "masters" which must greatly modify the system of slavery and ameliorate the condition of the slave. "Forbearing threatening." (Eph. vi, 9.) The word ἀνιέντες, rendered *forbearing*, I believe with Dr. Robinson signifies, in this place, "*to leave off, to cease from.*" The Christian master is not to *threaten* his servants. If not to *threaten* them, we may conclude, *à fortiori*, that he is not to use the lash. If harsh and threatening language is prohibited, certainly the severer discipline of blows is also forbidden. Forced service without physical punishment or threats would be an anomaly, and slavery without either would bear no resemblance to American slavery.

The various places in the Epistles in which the servant is exhorted to *obedience*, and to *render due reverence to his master*, have no bearing whatever upon the question of the right of slavery. St. Paul requires subjection to the civil authorities, but certainly cannot be supposed in this to sanction the despotic government of Nero and other tyrants. To require obedience to an unjust government is not to be understood as a sanction of its injustice.

In the study of the Scriptures we may be instructed as well by what is not found there as by what is. Now let it be observed that the *traffic* in slaves is a part of the system of American slavery. In all the slave states the two things have always gone together. Pious men have had some conscience upon the subject of breaking up families, and trading in slaves for merely mercenary purposes; but slaveholders in general, and many professors of religion among them, have not been so considerate. With them slaves have been a commodity to be disposed of merely for the benefit of the owner. My position is that buying and selling slaves is a part of the system of slavery as it exists in this country. It happens to be the fact, however, that not a word is said by the apostle upon the subject of the traffic in slaves. There are no directions given as to how slaves may be bought and sold *in a Christian manner*. This is one of the things not found in the New Testament, but which would most certainly have been found there if the traffic had been regarded as a legitimate Christian business.

What we have in the writings of Paul on the subject of the condition of servitude may well be considered as a reproof to those ultraists who consider slavery as sin *per se*, and who allow no circumstances to be taken into the account as modifications of the legal relations of master and slave, while it gives no sort of sanction to the system of slavery. All we have in the New Testament upon the subject is evidently designed to extract the evils from the system and to protect the slave. Under the influence of the salutary teachings of Christ and his apostles the system of servitude gradually lost its malignity, and finally only existed in the Church in name.*

The acts of the councils of the Church called *ecumenical*, for several centuries, on the subject of slavery, in nearly every instance were for the special benefit of the slave. No rule of discipline is found in the New Testament, no canon of any general council excommunicating a slaveholder, or requiring unconditional emancipation. One of the most popular American writers against slavery says that it is evident that the design of Christ and the apostles was to eradicate the evils from the system of slavery, and leave the framework to fall to pieces of itself.†

I conclude this discourse with objections to the system of slavery.

The system of human bondage, however modified, is inseparably connected with the slave-trade.

The domestic slave-trade, although much less offensive to humanity than the importation of slaves from Africa, is fraught with innumerable evils. Southern slave-owners, as a general thing, have ever been implicated in the traffic. Members of all the Churches have been in the habit of buying and selling "the bodies and the souls of men." Individual instances

---

* The reader will find the biblical argument pro and con in Dr. Van Dyke's fast-day sermon, and Prof. Tayler Lewis's reply. See Fast-Day Sermon; or, The Pulpit and the State of the Country.

† Key to Uncle Tom's Cabin.

have occurred which may admit of some palliation; few of these, however, can be justified by the Golden Rule. In general the purchase or sale of slaves is stimulated by mercenary motives. In cases of slaveholding which admit of the most favorable construction, such as possession by inheritance, or holding them in order to keep families together, the incidents of the system attach to the slave. When the owner dies, if his estate is solvent, his slaves are divided among his heirs at law. If he dies insolvent, his slaves are sold at auction to the highest bidder, with his other effects, for the benefit of his creditors.

The owner may treat his slaves with humanity and Christian kindness; but every hour he is liable to death, and that event will change the circumstances of his slaves, and may transfer them to cruel masters, and separate husbands and wives and parents and children for life. These consequences necessarily adhere to the fact of regarding slaves as property.

Admitting all that may be pleaded in behalf of humane and Christian masters, and it must be confessed there have always been many of these, the general fact is that in all the slave states men, women, and children have been exposed for sale like cattle in the market. The ancient Tyrians and the old Romans "traded in the bodies and souls of men," irrespective of nationality or caste; but it has been reserved for professed Christians to reduce an innumerable class of human beings to mere chattels, and to treat them as merchandise.

There is a more aggravated view which justice compels us to take of the slave-trade and of its relations to African slavery. The enslavement of the African race originated in stealing the poor Africans from their quiet homes and barbarously transporting them to foreign countries and selling them for slaves. At first the people found along the coast were kidnapped and carried off. After a while, to meet the demands of the market, the nearer tribes were induced to make war upon those more remote, take all the prisoners possible, and sell them to the slavers. This system occasioned an immense loss of life at the outset. A large per centage of those who were shipped died on the passage from a want of food, water, and air, while the remainder were sold into hopeless bondage.

That we may have something like an adequate idea of the terrible proportions of the African slave-trade, a few statistics will be in point. Up to 1787 ten millions of the African race had been sacrificed to this Moloch of professedly Christian nations, the slave-trade. "In 1768 the number of slaves taken from their homes amounted to 104,100. In 1786, 100,000. In 1807, the last year of the English slave-trade, it was shown by authentic documents, produced by the government, that from 1792 upward of 3,500,000 Africans had been torn from their country, and had either miserably perished on the passage, or been sold in the West Indies." *

I cannot now pursue this subject and give the statistics of the trade in Virginia and other slave states, during the progress of which the value of a slave increased from $25 to $1,500. The foreign slave-trade was prohibited by act of Congress in 1789, to take effect in 1808.†

It is quite enough for one of humane, not to say Christian, feelings to know that the enslavement of the African race originated in the nefarious slave-trade, to beget in his soul an abhorrence of the system of slavery as it has been practiced in the southern states. Those who brought the poor Africans from their peaceful haunts were "man-stealers," and those who bought them were parties to their enormous guilt. It was the market made for slaves in America that stimulated the trade, and that furnished the occasion for all the measures of barbarous cruelty which were incident to the slave-trade. If a man cannot purchase stolen goods, knowing them to be such, without involving himself in the guilt of the theft, how could the planter purchase negroes stolen from Africa, knowing them to have been stolen and forcibly brought away from their own country, without partaking of the guilt of man-stealing.

---

* The World's Progress: Slave-trade.
† For a glimpse at the horrors of the slave-trade, see Mr. Wesley's Thoughts on Slavery.

The African slave-trade has been proscribed by all civilized nations; but still so vital is it to the system of African slavery that, for several years, southern politicians have openly agitated the policy of reviving it in the southern states. Southern editors talked of it as a right, and advocated the idea of demanding of Congress the repeal of the act of that body proscribing it. The measure would possibly have been pressed but for the experiment of secession, by which the rebel states thought to secure the renewal of the slave-trade with other invaluable blessings.

Now who can consider the relations which exist between the system of slavery and the slave-trade, both domestic and foreign, without an utter horror of that system? That slavery originated in the slave-trade none will deny; and that it is kept in being by the same cause is equally indisputable. The effect of such a cause can but be bad. When I come to the conclusion that it is morally right to desolate a large portion of a continent, to sacrifice the lives of millions of human beings, in order to enslave millions more, I may conclude that African slavery is right.

The next objection which I bring against the institution of slavery is its cruel injustice to the slave.

> "He finds his fellow guilty of a skin
> Not colored like his own; and having power
> T' enforce the wrong, for such a worthy cause
> Dooms and devotes him as his lawful prey,
> And, worse than all, and most to be deplored

> As human nature's broadest, foulest blot,
> Chains him, and tasks him, and exacts his sweat
> With stripes, that Mercy with a bleeding heart
> Weeps, when she sees inflicted on a beast."
>
> COWPER.

If it would be injustice to deprive a man of one of his limbs, it would be a greater act of injustice to deprive him of all his limbs, and a greater act of injustice still to take possession of his whole body, but greatest of all to take possession of his mind, of his soul, of his immortality. What has the slave left to himself? He can think, he can pray; but he cannot appropriate his thoughts to his own advantage, he cannot pray audibly; he cannot lift up his voice in prayer without the consent of his master; he can attend no social gathering for religious purposes without his master's leave, and under the slave laws he is not allowed to meet an assembly of his own class without the presence of some white person appointed or authorized by his owner. The whole life, body, and soul is to be used for the advantage of the master, and is subject to his will or caprice. Can a slave fulfill the conditions of slavery and remain a man? Does not slavery degrade him from the dignity of human nature? Can it be otherwise than that he should be imbruted—should come as near to the level of a beast of burden as it is possible for a human being to be? If he is not a mere animal, or a tool, it is owing to the resistance of natural laws or moral forces which are in stern hostility against the necessary tendency of the condition of slavery; and so no thanks are due to the slave system if there is left in the slave a particle of the intelligence or the morality of manhood. If God's image is not spunged clean from the soul it is not because of any conservative power in slavery itself.

Now what more need be said to prove that slavery is the greatest crime that can be committed against humanity? What act of injustice can be imagined so flagrant, so heaven-daring, as making a human being a slave, or holding him in slavery? Is argument necessary to prove that it is unjust to take from a man or a woman his or her individual liberty, social life, and hopes; to annihilate the idea of family; to make marriage an impossibility; to make man a beast of burden, and woman an instrument of sensual indulgence, and of producing stock for the market. Is argument necessary here? Would it not be an insult to the intelligence of this age to attempt to prove by formal reasoning that slavery, in all ordinary circumstances, is a palpable violation of the rule which requires us to do to others as we would have them do to us? And this, with a Christian, is the rule of personal justice applicable to every human being.

I object to the system of human slavery, that its influence upon the slaveholder is "only evil continually."

Thomas Jefferson, a Virginian and a slaveholder, says, "There must be an unhappy influence on the manners of our people produced by the existence of slavery among us. The whole commerce between master and slave is a perpetual exercise of the most boisterous passions, the most UNREMITTING DESPOTISM on the one part and degrading submission on the other. Our children see this, and learn to imitate it. The man must be a prodigy who can retain his manners and morals undepraved by such circumstances." Again he says the masters are, by slavery, "transformed into despots."

Col. George Mason, also a Virginian, grandfather of James M. Mason of secession notoriety, says of the slaves, "They produce the most pernicious effect on manners. Every master of slaves is born a petty tyrant."

These are the sentiments of the southern statesmen of the olden time, delivered in grave debate, without passion; and who better know than they the influence of slavery upon both master and slave? If there were no other evidence of the demoralizing influence of slavery upon the master, an abundance is furnished in the present rebellion. The most fearful demonstrations of despotism and inhuman cruelty have marked the progress of the rebellion. The officers of the southern army are either slaveholders or are under the dictation of slaveholders. For their abandoned tyranny and remorseless cruelty, reference only need be had to their hanging hundreds of northern men, without judge or jury, upon mere suspicion of abolitionism, both before and since the commencement of the present war, the murders at Fort Pillow, and the treatment of Union prisoners in Libby prison in Richmond, at Andersonville, Georgia, and other places. These specimens of savage cruelty and barbarism truly explain the influence of slavery upon the heart of the master.

It is scarcely to be supposed that such a war as the war of the rebellion, still in progress, could ever have originated, and been so barbarously conducted, by any except a community of slaveholders.

The arbitrary rule of the Confederate authorities over the people of the rebellious states; their merciless conscription of all able-bodied men between sixteen and fifty-five; their denial of state rights to the states, a principle fundamental in southern policy; repudiating their securities; paying no respect to private property; neglecting to pay their soldiers, and robbing and starving the masses to feed and sustain the army, and committing innumerable other acts of misgovernment, all of which would disgrace the most heartless despotism the world ever saw, is further in evidence of the demoralizing influence of slavery upon the hearts and the social character of slaveholders.

I object to slavery that it is antirepublican.

If a republican form of government is best calculated to promote the greatest good of the greatest number, whatever conflicts with it is opposed to the general welfare, and ought to be opposed by all good citizens. Slavery is the assertion of the one-man power, and the maintenance of irresponsible authority. It admits no check or control of other persons or parties in the exercise of authority over the slave, or the disposition to be made of him. The slave can have no will; his law is the will of his master. The master, from his very childhood, is a "petty tyrant," as say Col. Mason and Mr. Jefferson; and how is he ever to become reconciled to a distribution of power as in a popular government? The participation of the masses in the affairs of government in the slaveholding states has always been merely nominal, while in small influential quarters there has always been a hankering for monarchical institutions. The facts accord with the philosophy of the spirit of slaveholding, and both show that it is at war with free institutions.

I object to slavery that it is at war with the spirit of the age.

The spirit of the nineteenth century is not merely the spirit of progress, it is the spirit of amelioration. The march of Christian civilization, of liberal principles, and of freedom, keeps pace with the progress of discovery and improvements in the arts. As discoveries in the sciences lighten the burdens of labor, so advancement in the philosophy of government and of social life places arbitrary power at a discount.

The doom of human slavery is sealed by the decision of the civilized world. It dies hard. Its struggles for existence increase in desperation as it approaches the period of its demise. The great American rebellion is one of its death spasms. In the struggle it shows great tenacity of life, and its friends and supporters clearly indicate the depth of their unnatural love for the great abomination by their willingness to sacrifice the nation's honor, if not her very existence, in its support. Slavery is with them so precious a thing that the unity, the peace, the treasure, and the most precious blood of a great nation are not too much to be put into the balance against negro slavery. The fanaticism of the southern fire-eaters is to be charged to the spirit of slavery, a spirit which struggles to stop the progress of society and to bring the world to a dead stand-still. While society is ascending slavery is descending. While the world is improving slavery is waxing worse. While humanitarian institutions are multiplying and accumulating power for good, and shedding light upon the dark places of the earth, slavery is blasting every green thing with its noxious vapors, and laboring to its utmost to shut out the light of heaven from millions of God's poor children.

Thanks be to God! the power of the institution is broken, the day of deliverance has come. The proclamation of President Lincoln, which proclaimed freedom to all the slaves within the rebellious states, ushered in a grand jubilee. One half of the four millions of African slaves in the United States by that beneficent measure are now restored to the dignity of manhood. The remaining two millions, with God's blessing upon the Union arms, will soon shake off their shackles and walk abroad upon the face of God's earth in the happy consciousness that, under God, they own themselves. The free Republic of America has been groaning under the burden of slavery since she began to be, and, although she was the first of the civilized nations which abolished the infamous slave-trade, slavery itself has been so deeply rooted in some of the states of the Union that she has been long in abating the nuisance, and finally it seems likely to die in the convulsions of a great slaveholders' rebellion.

Last, but not least, I object to slavery that it is opposed to the spirit of Christianity.

The great law of love, of doing to others as we would have them do to us, can only be reconciled to exceptional instances of slavery, and such cases would never arise if slavery were wholly abolished, and the slave-code annulled. What slave-owner would wish to change places with his human chattels? If not, in holding them in servitude does he love them as himself? Does he do by them as he would be done by? The condition of dependence and helplessness of the slaves does not change the state of the question, for the incapacity of large numbers of these poor creatures for self-support is the crime of slavery instead of its justification. Slavery has kept the colored race in a depressed and degraded condition; and it is bad logic to argue that, as the slaves are not able to take care of themselves, it is a Christian charity to keep them in slavery, that they may be taken care of by their masters. Nothing is more certain in the history of civilization than that if an enslaved race be invested with liberty, they will very soon take care of themselves.

The principles of Christianity settle the question of the unity and equality of the human race. "God hath made of one blood all nations of men for to dwell on all the face of the earth." In harmony with this divine truth is the great truth asserted in the Declaration of Independence, that all men are created free and equal. What right, then, has one man to restrain the liberties of another man of the same blood, who has as fair a claim to liberty as himself? Christianity enforces justice and brotherly kindness, and in no case furnishes an excuse, much less a justification, for exacting the toil and sweat of a fellow-creature without compensation and without his consent. That the strong should oppress the weak is not tolerated by the spirit and maxims of the Gospel; and that a man should buy and sell his brother man as he would buy and sell an ox is a thing perfectly abhorrent to all the principles of the New Testament. Slavery, in its spirit and form, is antichristian. It desecrates the image of God, and insults heaven. The devil is a slaveholder, and why not leave him alone in his glory?

> I would not have a slave to till my ground,
> To carry me, to fan me while I sleep
> And tremble when I wake, for all the wealth
> That sinews bought and sold have ever earned.
> COWPER.

X.

A COMPROMISE REJECTED.

Now it came to pass, when Sanballat, and Tobiah, and Geshem the Arabian, and the rest of our enemies, heard that I had builded the wall, and that there was no breach left therein; (though at that time I had not set up the doors upon the gates;) that Sanballat and Geshem sent unto me, saying, Come, let us meet together in some one of the villages in the plain of Ono. But they thought to do me mischief. And I sent messengers unto them, saying, I am doing a great work, so that I cannot come down: why should the work cease, whilst I leave it, and come down to you? Yet they sent unto me four times after this sort; and I answered them after the same manner.—Neh. vi, 1–4.

NATIONS have their rise and their decline. Sometimes they are convulsed and sustain great disasters, from which they recover and run a new race of prosperity. The holy land had been desolated by the captivity of its people in Babylon for seventy years. Conquering legions had profaned the soil which had been consecrated by miracles, had borne a long line of mighty kings, had been the subject of prophecies, and celebrated in sacred song. Holy memories were connected with every foot of the ground now desecrated and contemned. A vagabond population roamed over the sacred mountains, while the tombs of the kings and the temple of God were in ruins.

The period of the captivity had expired and the

time for reconstruction had come. Nehemiah, who was a member of the royal household at Shushan, was commissioned by royal proclamation to conduct a body of captive Jews to the site of the ancient city of Jerusalem, to rebuild the walls and re-establish the old institutions. Nehemiah was the president of the country, and was a man of great executive ability. He had great courage, great prudence, and a profound knowledge of human nature; and last, but not least, he was a man of much prayer and great faith in God. Such a man with such a commission, and such an object, it might have been supposed, would have enjoyed universal favor, and been crowned with uninterrupted success.

There was a mongrel mass of people scattered through the country that had been accustomed to have their own way, and they did not like the *puritan* rule of the new governor. They were Arabians, Ammonites, and Ashdodites. They had leaders, three of whom are named Sanballat, Tobiah, and Geshem. These leaders, and those who were their tools, we shall call *secessionists*. They were the open enemies of *President* Nehemiah and his administration, and they armed themselves and came up against him to give him battle. The president armed his men, however, and offered up prayer, for he believed both in fighting and in prayer.

The secessionists, finding it impossible to carry the president's works by open assault, had recourse to other expedients. They now affected to treat him and his party with great contempt. They called them feeble Jews, and said that if a fox should go up, he would break down their stone walls. The men were nothing but "greasy mechanics" and "mudsills." They are a pack of fanatics in religion, are unskilled in war, and are mere bunglers in building walls and towers, and one of our chivalry will chase five of them out of the country. Just look at them, praying and working and fighting. Now, as for ourselves, we don't pray much; we curse and swear and never work, but we fight; we are brave warriors, and we will give them the steel, a little taste of which will be quite sufficient to make them flee.

All these measures failing, the secession leaders then had recourse to another expedient. They now invite an armistice. They propose to President Nehemiah a friendly meeting "in some one of the villages in the plain of Ono." Lay down your weapons, say they, stop your work, and meet us on neutral ground, and let us see if our differences cannot be compromised. Come on now, we are brethren, why inclose your sacred city by a strong wall? Why treat us as sinners above all other men? Why continue this "fratricidal war?" President Nehemiah said to himself, "they think to do me mischief," and he gave them that noble answer which has been the admiration of all succeeding ages. "I am doing a great work, so that I cannot come down: why should the work cease while I leave it and come down to you?" They were not satisfied until they had "sent four times after this sort," while the president " answered them after the same manner." A most obstinate man was President Nehemiah, and quite stereotyped in his phraseology withal.

So ended the question of a compromise. The proposition was exceedingly plausible, and the answer was no doubt talked of by the secessionists and their sympathizers as captious and belligerent. The old president was considered pertinacious and uncharitable. The question of the armistice was settled, but the untiring secessionists were not content to leave the president to go on with his work of reconstruction.

The next measure was to accuse the president with a design to set up a kingdom of his own and to rebel against the legitimate government. Lies are the usual resort of interested politicians. This was a most insulting falsehood and slander, but was of a piece with all the other proceedings.

The last effort was to send an emissary to intimidate him, who advised him to shut himself up in the temple, and thus to save his life at the expense of his honor. His answer was: "Should such a man as I flee? And who is there, that, being as I am, would go into the temple to save his life? I will not go in." The president found that the messenger was a hired spy, employed by the secession leaders to frighten him out of his propriety, and thus destroy his influence.

Nehemiah was a man of a thousand. Neither force nor fraud, threats nor flattery, could jostle him a hair's breadth. With him duty was imperative; he could sacrifice his safety and his life, but he could not violate his conscience. The secession conspirators failed at every point, and were obliged to confess themselves totally vanquished.

In spite of the policy and power of the opposition, the work of reconstruction proceeded, and the old institutions were reared up; the old patriotism was revived, and prosperity gradually returned.

We have seen the main points of a most extraordinary case, one which is exceedingly suggestive, and which we shall now proceed to apply to our national affairs.

A portion of the country has been desolated by the ravages of war, not waged by a foreign foe, but by a portion of the people against the legitimate government—a rebellion instituted and carried on for ambitious ends, and without the least provocation. The simple point to which I invite attention now is that whole states have been overrun and ravaged by war. Agriculture and commerce have been destroyed, populous towns and cities desolated, and fertile fields rendered utterly barren.

The legitimate government has been engaged for

more than three years in the arduous work of restoring the majesty of the laws, the civil institutions of the country, and the peace and good order of society. As the rebellion, which is armed and aggressive, has been the source of all this evil, it was to be put down by force before order could be restored, or the shattered institutions of the rebellious states could be repaired and re-established. The first measure of the government was to reclaim the rebellious states. The rebellion had assumed the form and character of a great military despotism, and standing in the way of the beneficent objects of the government, it must first be put down. The war is a war for civilization, for law and order, for constitutional liberty, for the defense and preservation of the nation's life.

The rebels have done all they could to isolate themselves from the nation's heart, and to assume the attitude of foreigners and enemies. They ignore their national relations, and turn their back upon the old flag. They become the *Arabians*, the *Ammonites*, and *Ashdodites*, waging every sort of war against good old Nehemiah, who is hard at work, day and night, at the broken walls of the glorious old union.

Their leaders are cunning men, and as wicked as they are cunning. *Sanballat* of Richmond, *Tobiah* of New York, and *Geshem* of Ohio have enrolled and armed their forces, and by open assaults, flank movements, and profound strategy have sought to defeat the good work of restoration. "Cursed be their anger, for it was fierce, and their wrath, for it was cruel." These three are great leaders, and their effort is to make all the Arabians, Ammonites, and Ashdodites affect to believe that the wall can never be rebuilt, and that it will be much better to leave it as it is, then their hordes can overrun the sacred soil without hinderance. Every people, they say, have a right to be independent, and to govern themselves. The government of the old *puritanic* hypocrite who fasts and prays so much is a downright usurpation, and, to the chivalry, it is insufferable. We want *Sanballat* for our king; we do not believe in a government by majorities, a thing which our great man of Richmond says is an impossibility, and never existed in fact. And who knows better how the people have been fooled into the idea of self-government than the great political magician who now leads at his pleasure eight millions of people; who binds them in chains of adamant, and then has the impudence to tell them that they are free? Ah, *Sanballat* has long known how to manage the *Ashdodites* of the South, and the Ammonites and the Arabs of the North. He used to talk of the sacredness of the ballot-box and the government by constitutional majorities with the eloquence of Mercurius, but now that he has got the people of his sublime kingdom under his feet, he tells them plainly that they *never were anybody*, and the boasted theory of government by majorities is a farce. But those *Ashdodites* especially are a most glib set of talkers and deceivers.

The enemies of reform and reconstruction, like the enemies of Nehemiah of old, resort to taunts and gibes. This is an abolition and a black republican war, a nigger war, brought on by a pack of fanatics. The Yankees of the North have arrayed themselves against the chivalry of the South. "What will these feeble Yankees do?" Will they make an end in a day? Do they think to conquer the South with their mercenary hordes? And will they do this at a single blow? They are an ignoble race, wholly unable to cope with the chivalry of the South. There is no nobility in northern blood; the men are "greasy mechanics," and the women "factory girls;" their ruling idea is money-making. If they fight it is because they can make money by it. We Southerners are from the "Latin races." The Yankees are from the ignoble Puritan stock; we hate them, we contemn them, we will never be united with them in the same government again. Robert Toombs, the very pink of the Southern chivalry, is reported to have said that there were two reasons why the South would never be united again with the North: one was original sin, and the other the landing of the pilgrims on Plymouth Rock. I say nothing of the common sense of this statement, but introduce it only for the purpose of showing that even a great southerner can talk like a fool. There is the bitterness of gall in the very nonsense and affected pleasantries of these "descendants from the Latin races."

The rebels at the South and their sympathizers at the North laugh at the reverses of our arms, and depreciate all our successes, as well as grieve over them. A speaker in the Chicago Convention said, "For over three years Lincoln has been calling for men and they have been given. But with all the vast armies placed at his command he has failed, failed, failed, failed! Such a failure had never been known: such destruction of human life had never been known since the destruction of Sennacherib by the breath of the Almighty." And for this the President is called "a felon," "a monster," is charged with "perjury and larceny," and the army is called "his slaughter-pen." From sneers and gibes these *Ammonites* and *Arabs* proceed to vile abuse, and from overstrained statements to the most unblushing falsehoods. Hear them shout when our army meets with reverses. "Aha," they say, "so would we have it." And when our brave men drive the enemy before them and scatter them "like the chaff of the summer threshing floor," they shake the head and curl the lip and express grave doubts.

Now if what some of these enemies to the government say be true, who is responsible? If the government had failed to put down the rebellion so signally as the famous Chicago orator asserts, should it not have the advantage of the extenuating circumstances that a powerful party of sympathizers with the South have done what they could to bring about this very failure? In Congress they voted against supplies in men and money; and the Supreme Court of Pennsylvania issued an injunction to prevent the draft in the state, and so far as the example would go to prevent it also in other states, and thus to cripple the army. But for this party of sympathizers at the North one half of the blood which was spilled might have been spared, and we might long since have had an honorable peace. A beautiful specimen of consistency this for the men who have done their utmost to protract the war by weakening the hands of the government, to talk about the war's being a failure, and to groan over the blood that has been shed.

Then they endeavor to draw the government into an armistice, with the view to offer terms of peace to the rebels.

In their efforts for an armistice the Ashdodites, the Ammonites, and the Arabs are *confederate* parties; not "confederate states," but confederate *clans*. Old Sanballat of Richmond keeps behind the screen.

He says that "amnesty applies to criminals, but we have committed no crime."

What he proposes to demand is that the federal government should withdraw its armies from the insurgent states, and then he will condescend to treat with it on equal terms. There is no doubt, however, but that *Tobiah* of the city of Gotham, and *Geshem* of the Buckeye state, are under the instructions of the wily Sanballat, and that he would rejoice greatly if they could secure an armistice. Witness the Niagara peace measures. The President was invited to an interview in the plain of Ono. Ono? he demanded, and answered O no! I wont! albeit I will listen to and respectfully consider anything coming to me from the Confederate government, premising that no offer of peace that will save slavery will be accepted. "Insulting!" answered the sham legate from the South, and the Niagara peace negotiations ended. Still there is much talk among the Ammonites and Arabs of an armistice, and peace on the ground of mutual concessions. Come down "to one of the villages in the plain of Ono." O no, answered the pertinacious old Nehemiah. "I am doing a great work so that I cannot come down; why should the work cease while I leave it and come down to you?"

The great work in which the government is engaged is that of subduing the rebellion and of restoring government, and of establishing law and order in the southern states. The grand difficulty in leaving this work for an hour is that the reason for leaving it at all would be a reason for abandoning it finally. An armistice to rebels in arms? What for? To receive their submission? The door to this has never been closed. No armistice is necessary to secure this end. Is it then to treat with them that the armistice is urged? What would this be but to give up all that we are contending for, and granting all that the rebels claim? The very idea of an armistice implies one of two things: either that the rebels have rights, as such, to be considered and accorded, or that the government is unable to conquer them, neither of which can be conceded without utter ruin. The Ammonites and Arabs, in a grand council recently held at Chicago, maintained both of these propositions, and upon them built their peace platform.

In the Chicago Convention Captain Rynders said "he had heard one of the speakers state that the people of the South were traitors, which were very harsh words, as the people of the South were as brave and chivalrous a people as ever were put on the earth." Judge Alexander said, "We had tried the bayonet and had failed." So according to Captain Rynders and Judge Alexander the South have done no wrong, and we are unable to subdue them, and therefore we ought to have an armistice, and form a treaty of peace with them. In furtherance of this end the convention nominated a *war* candidate for president. And he acted upon the principle asserted by old senator Benton, that "platforms, like ipecac, are made to be swallowed and then thrown up again." He swallowed the whole, then threw up a part of it; but it seems probable will be, nevertheless subservient, so that all the Ammonites and Arabs will give him a united vote. In the mean time old Nehemiah will go on with his work until his commission runs out, when it is hoped by many of the good people who are in love with the institutions of the country that he may be commissioned again.

Since this wicked and barbarous war was commenced by the bombardment of Fort Sumter, there has never been a time in which an armistice on the part of the government would not have been both foolish and false to the interests of the country; but the impolicy, cowardice, and wickedness of the thing are more glaring now than ever. In what appears to be the end of the final struggle, when victory perches upon our banners at every great point of the conflict, is it a time to talk of an armistice and peace with the rebels? Sherman has just ended a most glorious campaign, is in the possession of Atlanta, "the gate of the South." Farragut has possession of the forts which defend Mobile, and Sheridan has driven Early out of the Shenandoah. When Lee's army before Richmond receives the shock of a general battle, there will be but little more to be done in order to conquer a permanent peace.

The alacrity with which men have volunteered to augment the army since the last call was made is an evidence of the disposition of the people to fight the rebellion down. The rebel sympathizers have been accustomed for the last few months to tell us that enlistments were played out, and that the people would not endure another draft. The statement is falsified by facts. The army never was reinforced with greater facility and never with better men than at the present time. Our army is more numerous and more efficient to-day than it has ever been since the commencement of the rebellion. The people say that this slaveholders' rebellion shall be put down, and if it is not put down it is evident enough that the failure must be attributed to the weakness of the government, and not to the want of patriotism in the people.

The supporters of the peace platform are quite zealous for the interests of religion, and become the admonitors of the clergy. They put on pious airs and tell us that our holy religion is a religion of peace, and hence all true Christians ought to use their influence in favor of "an armistice," and "peace on any terms." A ruffian assails you in a dark alley and points a dirk at your breast; you parry the weapon and raise your cane to level him to the ground, but he interposes: "Hold, my friend, are you not a Christian? Has not the Saviour told you not to resist evil? The religion of the Saviour is a religion of peace." "All right," answers the assailed party; "in my haste I parried your blow; I should have allowed you to pierce my breast and then have turned around and invited you to bury the deadly steel in my back also." This is a specimen of the peace theology. Let it be recollected that the same great teacher who said "resist not evil," said upon another occasion, "He that hath no sword let him sell his garment and buy one," hereby teaching us that there are occasions upon which it is lawful to take the sword. And if there ever was such an occasion the present wicked rebellion furnishes one.

Christian ministers are severely censured by the peace men for their encouragement of the war to put down the rebellion. They are told that ministers of the Gospel should be men of peace. True, but some of us think that the only way to have an honorable and a Christian peace is to put down the rebellion.

The last day of thanksgiving was noticed by the Mayor of the city of New York, who took occasion in advance to admonish the clergy of the city to preach on that occasion in favor of peace, and to pray for peace, and thus to keep within the terms of their holy commission. I suppose the clergy proceeded upon the presumption that they understood their own business as well as Mayor Gunther did. Thank God the pulpit is yet free! Some suppose that a minister has no business to say one word in favor of the government. St. Paul did not think so. To enforce obedience to the civil authorities is a part of the duty of the pulpit, whatever party politicians may say. They may try to badger the clergy into their notions of an unconditional peace, but they will lose their labor.

We have had an abundance of cant from politicians of a certain stamp upon "political preaching,"

and "the clergy entering the arena of politics."
There doubtless is a line of propriety which governs
this subject which a clergyman should not cross, yet
there are multitudes of so-called peace men who do
not discern where this line is. A certain preacher
not long since in a sermon quoted the words of St.
Paul, in the 13th of Romans, "Let every soul be subject to the higher powers," etc., when, before he had
made a remark, one of our sensitive souls took himself away with evident indignation at hearing politics
introduced into the pulpit. With him the language
of St. Paul was downright abolitionism. Another
illustration will show how little of conscience there
is in this carping about "clerical politicians." A
noted politician was accustomed to say from the
stand, "Let the clergy attend to their own peculiar
functions, and leave politics to laymen." But in
process of time he wanted the help of a Roman Catholic priest in a canvass, and he invited the good
father upon the stand to make a speech. The speech
was made and he cheered the father lustily. This
was proof positive that it was not the fact of clergymen's entering the political arena that so horrified the
gentleman, but the fact that they are not on his side.
I find that clergymen who stand upon the peace platform are very acceptable to our peace politicians;
but, thank Providence, there are not many of them.
Let us have peace, but let us have it on principles
which will give it unfailing stability.

A part of the plot against President Nehemiah was to accuse him of a treasonable design to make himself a king. The same slander is often heard from the lips of the Ammonites and Arabs of our times against our modern Nehemiah. It has often been said that President Lincoln intends to establish a despotism in the country—ay, that he had already set up a despotism. In the Chicago Convention it was said, "They talk of a rebellion in the South; but a greater rebellion has been in progress in the North." The same charge of subverting constitutional liberty is brought against the administration in the debates of the aforesaid convention in a variety of forms.

It is assumed in the platform adopted by that convention, that the President is likely to interfere with the freedom of the elections through the military force. To all these shameful slanders the President may answer as did Nehemiah of old: "There are no such things done as thou sayest, but thou feignest them out of thine own heart." It is astounding to see how far prejudice and party zeal will go. For party ends the most improbable things, and even impossibilities, are asserted as facts, with an appearance of sincerity by persons who on other subjects are governed by the ordinary principles of common justice and common sense.

Finally, some have endeavored to frighten good old Nehemiah by threats of personal violence. They say to him, "Remember the ides of March." "First ballots, and if they do not answer, .then bullets." "You had better abdicate your seat, or it will be pulled out from under you." To all this he answers, "Shall such a man as I flee?" No, Nehemiah, not yet. It will be time enough for you to leave the work of restoring the Union when the people so decide by their votes. Resting on the strong arm of the true-hearted people, and the protection of the stronger arm of God, you may defy the malicious acts of all traitors and rebels.

XI.
NO NEUTRALITY.

Curse ye Meroz, said the angel of the Lord, curse ye bitterly the inhabitants thereof; because they came not to the help of the Lord, to the help of the Lord against the mighty.— Judges v, 23.

The history of the Judges marks a peculiar period. Three great leaders had preceded this period, and the government had been uniform. After these succeeded the Judges, who administered the government, some for brief and others for longer periods. They were generally called in an extraordinary manner, and constituted no part of a line of succession, according to the law of pedigree.

One of these Judges was a woman, a prophetess. During the administration of Deborah, the children of Israel were sorely oppressed by Jabin king of Canaan. Twenty years of sore servitude under a mighty tyrant had ground down the people, and well nigh broken their spirit. Still they had confidence in the prophetess, and some faith in God. Jabin had nine hundred chariots of iron, and an innumerable host of warriors; but being summoned to the field in the name of God, ten thousand of the children of Naphtali and Zebulon followed Deborah and Barak. The battle was joined, and the Canaanites were scattered like the chaff before the wind, and the whole host was cut off, so that there was not a man left. Sisera fled, on foot and alone, to a small piece of neutral territory occupied by Heber the Kenite, and was there slain by Jael with a nail and a hammer.

Then Deborah composed a song, which is marked by great poetic beauty and power. She celebrates the victory, makes mention of the instrumentality employed, but gives all the glory to God. The text is a part of this song, but somewhat variant from the general strain. It is an imprecation upon a community who took no part in the battle.

Meroz was a city or a district which probably lay near the battle-field, and upon the inhabitants of which lay special obligations to take an active part in the struggle for liberty. The people preferred their own ease and safety to the obligations and honors of patriotism and religion, and so stayed at home, while the pious and the brave dared to fight, and were rewarded with the honors of a glorious victory. Meroz was cursed, and went into oblivion. Now, no one is so wise as to know even its locality. A terrible lesson this to neutrals in a great moral struggle.

With these preliminaries I shall proceed to the consideration of the lessons suggested by the history.

God and Satan, Heaven and Hell, Government and Rebellion, are engaged in a mighty struggle.

What should we do in this great conflict?

It is our duty to take ground decidedly and publicly for our country and the right.

We are all concerned in the issue of this great battle of principles, and have responsibilities to meet in relation to it, and consequently our adherence should be promptly and publicly given. A man who would do his duty as a Christian or a patriot must not try to do it in secret. Nicodemus came to Christ by night, probably to avoid publicity. An awakened conscience should not court darkness, but seek the day. What is there in the matter of moral responsibility to be ashamed of? The question is simply a question of right; and who should be ashamed to do right? And who should hesitate in a question of plain duty? It is cowardly, it is weak and mean to skulk when conscience speaks out plainly. In such a case cowardice is criminal, and to be noncommittal is a sin against God. A stand must be made. A public commitment is the first condition of discipleship and of citizenship.

Active service is required of every member of the Church and of the State.

The world, the flesh, the devil, and the rebels are in active opposition to God and us. They are only to be overcome by prompt and stout resistance. No compromise must be made with these foes; there must be no relaxation in our efforts, no faintness in our spirit, until they are finally put to flight.

Religion and patriotism are not the mere absence of overt acts of iniquity and treason; they constitute a grand controversy, a lifelong fight. Passiveness in this cause is as much out of place as it would be in a soldier amid the roar of battle, or in a sailor during a storm at sea. Action, onward, aggressive action, is the only appropriate course and the true line of duty. All hell is in motion. The devil goes about like a roaring lion, hunting the souls of men, and shall we sleep? The enemy is upon us, and shall not we arise and shake ourselves? The foe thunders from afar, and shall not we shout for the battle?

We should hazard all upon the stake. Too much cannot be sacrificed for the prize which is in controversy; too much cannot be done in the service which is required. All our powers should be brought into this work.

All we have and are should be laid upon the altar. The man who found the pearl of great price went and sold all that he had and bought it, and was infinitely the gainer by the transaction. The duty in question is paramount, and nothing is too much to give or to do in such a cause. Time, property, ease, life itself, should be considered worthless in the comparison. Paul says, "I count all things but loss for the excellency of the knowledge of Christ Jesus my Lord;" "What shall it profit a man if he gain the whole world and lose his own soul?"

I shall next proceed to show the criminality of inaction.

It is the cause of God which requires active support.

It is "to the help of the Lord" that we are required to come. Not as though God were a weak party who requires aid to save him from superior strength, but he works by instrumentalities, and the instruments being a part of his plan are essential to its completeness, and their absence would be at least a defect, and might prove the cause of failure. God could carry on his work without the intervention of means, and could save it from failure by a miracle. But we have no right to look for any miraculous or extraordinary intervention in a case in which human agency constitutes one of the conditions of success.

God invites, yea, demands our help, and he has a right to command; nor could he confer a greater favor upon us than to embrace our agency in his plans of working. What contempt of his condescension and wisdom, what disobedience to his commands is inaction, or refusing to take the post assigned us in the great pending battle? The Church is God's militant host, his great fighting army. He demands that all enlist, and that all range themselves on his side; that all join in the battle and fight, fight valiantly, fight to the death under his banner.

The dearest interests are involved in the pending struggle.

Human interests are so united that we are in a measure made responsible for the well-being of others. No human being can be lost without involving others in fearful guilt. Cain repudiated his obligation to seek the welfare of his brother when he demanded, "Am I my brother's keeper?" The principle involved in this question is essentially anti-social; a denial of the relations and mutual obligations of man to man. In opposition to this principle of selfish individuality, this presumption of isolation from the interests of the world around us, it is true that, by an unchangeable law, we are under obligations to all other men precisely in proportion to our power to serve their interests. When we are able to do anything for the benefit of a fellow-being we are responsible to God and to society for doing that thing, and are involved in criminality to the extent of its importance to the interests of the individual and the world, if we, for any cause whatever, neglect or decline doing it. It is no light thing that God has put the dearest interests of others within our power. If the souls of men and the existence of the country are at stake, it is a fearful hazard; and if we are made answerable for their salvation, on us rests a tremendous responsibility.

Thus far in this discussion I have considered both spiritual and secular interests to be in imminent peril; both assaulted, and both seeking for help. God is interested in both, and we are responsible for the security of both. That the world is not better is, in part at least, our fault. Its errors, vices, and ruin may be laid at our door. What countless interests are at stake in the moral world, and calling us to the rescue!

What shall be said of the condition of the country, and the call upon every citizen for sympathy and prompt action? What shall be said of him who ignores his obligations and does nothing? What more pitiable instance of selfishness and cowardice can be imagined than one who enjoys the protection of the state, and yet takes neutral ground while great principles and interests are at stake, as in the present struggle? Constitutional liberty is threatened; the commerce of the world is in peril; vast armies are reaping the fields of death; the wail of widows and the cry of orphans, like the noise of the restless sea, are wafted upon every breeze, and the sound is waxing louder and louder. Our country's life is in peril; our country's life is in peril of being smitten out forever! The nation is suffering a fearful agony, and is threatened with a death-spasm. Under emergencies so terrible, who will fold his arms, or ask to be excused from active participation in the responsibilities, labors, and sacrifices of the fearful crisis which is upon us?

A fearful array of strength is to be met and overcome.

It was "against the mighty" that the inhabitants of Meroz refused to array themselves. To a coward this might be a reason why he should avoid participation in the contest, but to a true soldier and a patriot it would be an urgent reason for instant and persevering action. The greater the resources of the foe in numbers, skill, and treasure, the greater the reason why he should be met with all the strength which can be brought into the field. All should fight, and fight with a will, lest the good cause fail through the weakness of its defenders.

The world, the flesh, and the devil are combined against the government of God and the kingdom of Christ. Mighty foes these; a most fearful combination against the hopes and interests of humanity. All the enginery of hell is brought into the field. The world, with its charms and false showing; the flesh, with its gratifications; the devil, with his wiles and fiery darts, are ready for the onset. The battle is begun, the citadel of the soul is to be taken by assault. See the marshaled hosts; hear the shouting of the captains. The clarion sounds loud and shrill. Now cowards fly, but brave men and true rush into the fray. Their language is, "Shall such men as we flee?" The hotter the battle the higher mounts their courage; the greater the hazard, the greater their enthusiasm, and the harder their blows; the more numerous and powerful the foe, the more energy and skill and might they bring to the battle.

When the cause is a good one, the craft and power

of the opposition are reasons why no true man should avoid the conflict. When the emergency is pressing, when all that we value is in danger, when the foe is mighty, then is the hour which reveals the meanness of spirit and the heartless cowardice, or the treachery of those who come not to the help of the Lord. The very state of things which causes them to keep out of sight, that they may be out of danger, will in the final day cover them with infamy and sink them in perdition. What will it then avail the delinquent to say, "It was a terrible foe which I was summoned to meet. I was afraid. I love an easy and quiet life." Ah, the Judge will then say, "Out of thine own mouth will I condemn thee. Was the foe mighty! So much the greater the demand for valiant soldiers. Wast thou afraid? Go and contend with the devouring flames. Didst thou seek thine ease when God's hosts were arrayed on the battle-field? Go away and lie down in sorrow. 'Thou camest not to the help of the Lord, to the help of the Lord against the mighty.'" There is the grand point of their baseness and their criminality.

Deliberate neutrality is, in some cases, the basest species of treason. It shows a heart of enmity, where there is not courage and manliness enough to take the place of an open foe. Shall such enemies be exempt from the fate of avowed rebels? Shall they not rather be considered worthy of special marks of disapprobation? Shall they not be punished both **for** their heartlessness in the cause and their hypocritical professions of love for it?

In the final judgment, as Christ describes it, those who are cursed and banished are not charged with overt acts of rebellion, but with the want of positive qualities, the fruits of active piety. They may have been willing that the hungry of God's little ones should be fed, and the naked should be clothed; they may often have said, "Be ye warmed and be ye filled," but this is not enough. They are banished into everlasting fire because they are not found active and faithful in serving God. The absence of open hostility to the cause of God and religion is the vail by which they try to cover a heart so base as to seek the friendship of both parties, so destitute of the love of God as to court the favor of mammon. All such will have their portion with the devil and his angels.

From what has been presented, it will appear that inaction, in the great question of duty to God and society, is highly criminal. Let us now look at the consequences.

The punishment which will be inflicted upon those who prove recreant.

The curse ordered to be pronounced upon Meroz was both judicial and prophetic. It was ordered by "the Angel;" probably "the Angel of the Covenant" is to be understood, the Angel who led the children of Israel through the wilderness, who appeared to Joshua, who fought for God's people and discomfited their enemies.

The curse includes—

Disgrace.

To be disapproved by God is to be dishonored in the most fearful sense, and without the possibility of escape. The scorn of the multitude can be borne, but the frown of God withers all the laurels of men, and covers them with shame. God says, "They that despise me shall be lightly esteemed."

There is also the loss of power.

The wicked lose the power which they once had of winning fame and a name of doing good or great things. The talent is taken from "the unprofitable servant," who "hid it in the earth." He may not have injured it: he may say, "There thou hast that is thine." It is all there safely concealed, and it can be promptly returned. But the lord of that servant says, "Take the talent from him." The barren fig-tree cursed by the Saviour was, from that moment, "dried up from the root:" thenceforth it was without the power of yielding fruit—a fit emblem of a fruitless member of the Church of God, or of an able-bodied man who refuses to face the foe. Buried talents are useless, and will by and by be taken away and given to the faithful and earnest worker, where they will be turned to some account. Sloth and narrowness of mind are in the first instance chosen as privileges and blessings, but in the end they are judicial inflictions. "The sluggard will not plow by reason of the cold, therefore shall he beg in harvest and have nothing." He has chosen idleness, he shall therefore be cursed with the eternal blight of all his powers and privileges. He assumed the position of a mere negative, he is therefore condemned to be one; to be good for nothing, and have nothing, and be nothing.

The curse implies divine wrath, without mitigation and without end.

We may gather some intimations of the meaning of the curse in the text from the fact that the place where lived the people so fearfully cursed is wholly obliterated from the geography of the world. The last we hear of it is, "Curse ye Meroz, saith the Angel of the Lord, curse ye bitterly the inhabitants thereof, because they came not to the help of the Lord, to the help of the Lord against the mighty." The subsequent history of this delinquent people is shrouded in darkness. Who can bless whom the Lord curses? What power can deliver us out of his hands, if he sends down his wrath upon us? The curse of God is a thunderbolt of vengeance, hurled at the transgressor, sinking him in outer darkness. That curse is the worm that never dies—the fire that never shall be quenched. It is weeping, wailing, and gnashing of teeth. It is remorse, despair, and endless night; starless, moonless night. And what a doom awaits the sinner when ends this gracious day of visitation! Now he hopes for impunity; then his hopes will all die. Now he has Christian sympathies; then he shall be eternally shut out from Christian associations.

The subject is fruitful of practical suggestions.

No favor to a good cause is of any value but that which is practical.

In a great struggle, of what value is passive favor? The people of Meroz might have had many good wishes for the success of Deborah and Barak in the great battle which was to take place; but of what avail were their good wishes when hard blows alone were to decide the fate of the whole people? What weight has a community of neutrals in a war for national existence? They may be numerous, wealthy, and influential, but if they will furnish neither men nor means for the contest, of what value are they to the state? Ten thousand, or ten hundred thousand such citizens would not be equal to one genuine patriot.

We ask not for good opinions and fair words, but we want brave hearts, noble daring, deeds which tell, blows which will strike terror into the heart of the enemy, an onward movement which will break their ranks, scatter their hosts, and take their citadels. Action, action is what the exigences of the cause require. We ask you not what you secretly think of these things, but what you will do? What ground will you take? What sacrifice will you make? What danger will you face? What estimate do you put upon the cause? Where action is duty, inaction is sin. What defense would it be for an idle servant to plead that he had not wasted your goods, nor destroyed the products of your field? Shall an able-bodied citizen, whose services are required in times of national peril, answer the charge of refusing to obey the call of his country by pleading that he has not given aid and comfort to the enemy, he has not been secretly confederate with the foe? Will that meet the case? Will it be a valid ground of justification against the accusation of delinquency in duty to the government? Fancy a sinner coming up to the judgment-seat and pleading, " Lord, I always wished well to the cause of religion. I never reviled or persecuted thy servants. I was not a murderer nor a thief, nor a profane swearer, nor a Sabbath-breaker, nor a libertine, nor a drunkard. Now what have I done that I should be condemned?" Would not the answer be, " What have you done that you should go to heaven? What kind of a steward have you been? Did you take the office with the understanding that you were to do nothing?" Such pleas are often made here, but they will not answer before the bar of God.

You may be an inoffensive creature, trying to do no harm. This is not all that is required. If you have none of the positive elements of Christian character it is folly for you to count yourself a Christian.

You neither go into battle nor "abide by the stuff." You neither fight, nor strengthen those who do. You occupy the place of a mere sponge: absorb all and give out nothing. If you could be saved in this way the credit would all redound to others. Do you desire to be saved thus? Would you have the Church do all for you, and you do nothing for her? O shame! where is thy blush? You are a sinner, and a great sinner, and God will so write you down in the day of judgment. The unprofitable servant will be cast into outer darkness.

These times eminently call for the spirit of aggression.

The enemy is upon us, and there is no safety but in a forward movement and a decisive victory. There is no such thing as standing still. The tide of iniquity is every day gathering force; inaction is certain destruction. National sins, individual sins, sins in high places and in low, call aloud for instant and continued action, energetic, aggressive action. We are to conquer or be conquered; to fight bravely and win a glorious victory, or be ingloriously defeated and driven from the field. O for a simultaneous movement upon the foe! O for the aggressive spirit of primitive times! May God give the victory!

The impossibility of neutrality is as evident in civil as in religious affairs.

The nation is engaged in a great war; a war of defense against a gigantic rebellion. There are but two sides to the question at issue. The unity and the very existence of the nation are on one side, and its dismemberment and ruin on the other. There is no middle ground. Kentucky made an effort at neutrality, but finally gave it up as impracticable. Many men at the North have tried to be on both sides, or on neither, but have failed. In all cases they have been found on the side of the rebellion. As Christ says, "He that is not for me is against me," so it is, he that is not for the government and the nation is against it. Neutrality is treason as truly in relation to our national interests as in religion.

Let those then who refuse to give active support to the government in this terrible crisis expect the curse which fell on Meroz of old. For if the cause of Deborah and Barak was the cause of God and truth, such also is the cause of the American Union.

XII.
NO FALSE PEACE.

THEY HAVE HEALED ALSO THE HURT OF THE DAUGHTER OF MY PEOPLE SLIGHTLY, SAYING, PEACE, PEACE; WHEN THERE IS NO PEACE.—Jer. vi, 14.

The word peace is understood to be used in the text for concord between parties. In this sense I shall use it. Some parties can never be at peace; it is naturally and morally impossible. The impossibility arises from the antagonism which exists between good and evil, truth and error. Under some circumstances an effort to make peace is to commence a war against God and nature. In cases in which hostility is the natural and moral condition of the parties, peace is neither desirable nor attainable. All efforts to harmonize invincible opposites are worse than foolish; they are so many assaults upon the laws of nature and the order which God has established.

This much being premised, I shall proceed to discuss the two opposites, false and true peace.

False peace.

This peace is hollow, wholly outward, a mere semblance. Where peace is nothing but a cessation of external hostilities it implies no radical agreement, and is likely to be interrupted on the slightest occasion. Such a peace is hollow but not empty. Like a bombshell, it may be fearfully dangerous.

At the present time much is said about making peace with the rebels. They desire peace; that is, they wish to be let alone. They want the privilege of casting off their allegiance to the government, of repudiating the Constitution, of robbing the treasury, of taking possession of our forts, ships of war, and navy-yards, and of erecting a government based upon slavery as "its chief corner-stone," and of being let alone in all this. They ask, "Why send your armies to invade our territory and destroy our property and kill our citizens? Why not grant us the boon of peace? Leave us in the peaceable possession of our rights; this is all we ask." And there are some among us who pretend to think this reasonable.

Were there no other objections to this plea for peace, I object to it that no substantial peace can be made with the leaders of rebellion. What basis for confidence is there in men who have broken faith with the government, and repudiated their oaths of office, and plundered the public property? What but a hollow peace could be made with such a class of men? With a frontier of thousands of miles, and endless jealousies growing out of the peculiar constitutions and commercial interests of the two sections, how long would a peace last which should include the recognition of southern independence?

Every vessel entering a southern port would be searched to see if colored persons were on board. Whatever stipulations for the free navigation of the Mississippi might be entered into, that river would not remain free for a twelvemonth. Every boat from the North on its return would be hailed and brought to a dozen times, to institute a search for contrabands. The constant recurrence of such irritating causes would soon bring on another war.

The idea that the United States can be divided and constitute two governments, and they maintain amicable relations with each other, is altogether Quixotic, and not to be entertained for a moment.

Equally hollow and shortlived would be any pacification of the present trouble founded upon a guarantee of a continuance and perpetuity of slavery. Slavery has been the great bone of contention from the first. It is bound either to rule or ruin. It will not consent to be stationary. It must be allowed to push itself everywhere, and overshadow everything near. It everywhere makes fight with the progress of liberal opinions, and with the advance of freedom. He must be blind indeed who supposes that slavery can be restored and protected by constitutional provisions, and yet peace be maintained between the supporters of slave and of free labor. The question is settled that human slavery in the United States must die. The people have so decreed. Indeed, already it is so nearly an accomplished fact that it is scarcely a question of debate. Those politicians who say, "Give back to the southern people their slaves, and guarantee to them their constitutional rights, and we will have peace," are a small company and are growing "beautifully less." There is now no light in this direction, if there ever was any. The day for such diplomacy has passed. The southern leaders themselves repudiate the idea of a return to the old Union upon the basis of constitutional guarantees for the protection of slavery. They say, "Our independence is what we are fighting for, and we are willing to sacrifice everything else to that; even slavery itself may go if it should stand in the way." By slavery they mean *their present slaves*, for if their independence were acknowledged it would not be long before they would be engaged in the slave-trade, and by that means would quickly replenish their empty slave-pens. Jefferson Davis and the southern editors may prate as much as they please about giving up slavery: they are slave-drivers at heart. If their slaves were all given up to-day, they would have more to-morrow if they could.

The wounds of the state cannot be healed by such nostrums as these.

A false peace is a dangerous peace.

A true peace is always safe. Any peace short of that which is based upon the submission of the rebels to the government must be fraught with peril. It would hazard our national life, on whatever terms the peace should be concluded. The only terms on which the rebels will consent to end the war is the acknowledgment of their independence. And how can this be done without peril to our own? Two independent nations in the same country, of the same language, the same religion, and the same political creed, are scarcely a possibility. Two nations, with such antagonisms as have grown up and been aggravated by civil war, not separated by natural barriers, must of necessity be at war with each other. Peace obtained on the condition of recognition would be the peace of a day, with endless hostilities beyond.

More than all this, as we should lose our power and prestige as a nation, we should be insulted and injured by the nations of Europe, and embroiled in wars with them, or obliged to submit to wrongs which we would be unable to avenge. Our safety lies in our power; our power once gone, we should be the sport of tyrants and despots the world over. Even second and third-rate powers would expect to infringe upon our rights with impunity.

A beautiful way this of securing peace! Better far would it be for us to continue the war for twenty years, or until our resources of men and money are utterly exhausted.

When we seek for peace to avoid the burdens of war, we should always ask ourselves what other danger will this peace bring with it? It would be of no avail to make peace with Satan in order to escape perdition.

A false peace is a wicked peace.

A peace made between contending parties at the expense of principle is sin. Lord Bolingbroke says, "All compromises are immoral." This is too sweeping a proposition. We may in some cases compromise a personal right; we may sacrifice something, yea, much, to the public good; we may compromise anything that is immaterial or morally indifferent; but we cannot sacrifice humanity or justice or religion for considerations of policy or worldly expediency without incurring guilt. Such compromises are indeed immoral. To make peace with the rebels upon any other ground than that of submission to the laws and the restoration of the Union, would be to concede the right of rebellion against lawful authority and just government. It would be not merely impolitic, it would be as wicked as the rebellion itself.

The wickedness of such a peace would be aggravated by several marked circumstances. In the first place, the government assumed at the breaking out of the rebellion that it was without any just cause, a high crime against Christian civilization and against society, and a sin against God; that it was destructive of civil government and public morals. On these grounds the administration justified itself before the world for defending itself by force and arms. On these grounds Christian citizens have taken up arms and marched into the field of deadly strife with a good conscience, and ministers and Churches have prayed to the God of armies for the success of our brethren. To make peace with the rebels now, without their submission, is to abandon this high ground, and to confess that the rebels are right and we are wrong. Should peace be declared without the submission of the rebels, only one thing could save the country from the guilt and shame of a wicked abandonment of her high moral position, and that would be the utter hopelessness of the Union cause. Should the federal forces be finally and fatally beaten, the claims of humanity might require us to abandon a hopeless struggle, and to recognize the rebels as an independent nationality. In such a case the character of the rebellion would be set aside in the necessities of a revolution. The present is no time for a resort to peace on any such grounds, and for any such reasons. For the last twelve months our arms have scarcely had a disaster worthy of mention. Victory upon victory has followed our brave boys, and now the power of the rebellion is narrowed down to a single point. Under present circumstances an act of pacification with the rebels could only be construed as a humiliating confession that the national cause is wrong. This would be a national apostasy from the principles of the Constitution and the grace of the revolution. It would be a shameful acknowledgment that the great American

Republic is unworthy of national existence, because it is too weak and cowardly to maintain it.

Another aggravation of the base compliance supposed would be the necessary and wicked waste of life and treasure which the war has occasioned. If the war is wrong now, it was wrong at first, and should never have been undertaken. If it has been wrong from its inception, then our government, with the approbation of nearly the whole Northern people, has causelessly and wickedly shed rivers of blood, and destroyed millions upon millions of treasure. If the war for the Union is wrong, then upon our souls, who have approved it and aided it, and not on the government alone, lies the blood not only of our slaughtered fellow-citizens who have perished in battle, but the blood of the hundred thousand rebels who have been sacrificed. Such are the logical consequences of a settlement of the present war upon any other terms than that of the submission of the rebels to the lawfully constituted authorities of the United States.

Another aggravation of the sin of a false peace is that it leaves a great emergency but partially met. The war was commenced on the part of the rebels for the perpetuation of slavery. On our part it necessarily became a war for freedom. The proclamation of the President liberated the slaves of the rebellious states so far as the arms of the United States carried their authority. This was the period;

this was the long-expected hour of release to hundreds of thousands of slaves. The logic of events proved that the successful prosecution of the war for the Union would be the means of the emancipation of the multitudes still in slavery. These poor creatures are now looking for the consummation of their cherished hopes, and the answer to their many prayers. Now just as this great object is upon the point of being gained, at the very moment the residue of enslaved men and women are lifting the cup of liberty to their lips, shall it be dashed to the ground? God forbid. President Lincoln has constantly refused to listen to any terms which did not include the restoration of the Union and freedom for the slaves; and an abandonment of this position would "break hope to the heart" after giving it to the ear. It would parry and turn away a grand stroke of Providence; it would partially beat down one of the most glorious achievements of the ages; it would destroy the faith and blast the hopes which the policy of the government and its past successes have inspired.

Finally, the nation is suffering from a grievous "hurt" or wound inflicted by the rebellion, and the business of the war is to probe it to the bottom, cleanse it, and prepare it for a radical cure. Will it not be both foolish and wicked to heal the surface and leave the consuming gangrene, the festering ulcer, to work its way to the vitals of the nation? To heal the wounds of the state slightly is to aggravate them, and to become in a measure responsible for the dire results which follow. This superficial healing has its agents and its advocates. There are an abundance of peace-mongers who cry, "Peace, peace." Just now these men are the most troublesome, if not the most dangerous class of people with whom the government has to contend. Let these empirics stand aside, and leave Gen. Grant and Gen. Sherman to cut the knot with their swords. Doubtless peace is desirable. We all want peace, but not a false peace. We want no hasty, transient peace which God does not sanction, and which will vanish in smoke. Let us hear no more of this unholy peace. Let not the people be deceived and disappointed by rumors of a sudden cessation of hostilities. Let us look for peace through the success of our armies in the field, and not by compromise.

The government will not abandon its high ground and yield to the unreasoning clamor of a few political demagogues through mere weariness of their noise. No peace which compromises with sin can be approved of Heaven. "First pure, then peaceable;" "the fruit of righteousness is peace;" are the divine maxims.

Having discussed the different kinds of false peace, I proceed to a brief notice of true peace.

True peace is that which "God has spoken" or authorized.

The peace which has the divine sanction is that which is conservative of the civil power.

God has spoken out unmistakably in favor of the maintenance of civil government, and especially of the citizen's duty to sustain it. Would he then approve of an abandonment of legitimate and just civil constitutions and systems of public law? Certainly not; we need no argument to prove this. God never contradicts himself. He has settled the question of the authority and the obligations of law and government finally and forever. Any peace which removes the stays and defenses of society and the public interests cannot meet with the divine approval. When God authorizes peace, it is a solid and lasting peace.

When a peace is settled between contending parties under the divine approval, no public interest is put in jeopardy.

God is a God of order, and not of confusion. Under his administration social and individual rights are held sacred. His government is just, as well as merciful. He never sanctions a weak leniency which endangers the public safety. There is no authority for setting at large thieves, robbers, and murderers out of sheer clemency. Mercy to the offender in such cases would be cruelty to the unoffending citizen. The same principles obtain in the adjustment of difficulties between contending parties, and in the administration of public law in dealing with state offenders. *Fiat justitia, ruat cœlum.*

Let it be distinctly understood that the government is not now called upon to make terms with a nation, nor with a *belligerent power*, as such a power is understood in the law of nations, but the question is one of *peace with rebels*. Now, in the name of reason and religion, what terms of peace can be made with rebels upon any other basis than that of submission to law and to the authority of the government? To give rebels against a just government the boon of reconciliation upon the condition of submission is Christian, is Godlike. To go beyond this, and grant conditions of peace without submission, would be a total abrogation of the dignity of the state. It would be the end of civil authority and of all just government. God has never "spoken" such a "peace" as this. Politicians may have contrived it, cowards may have spoken it, rebels may have demanded it, but no higher authority has given it sanction. · Patriots and Christians trample it under their feet.

A true peace is one which establishes law and government, and stamps rebellion with infamy.

After the fearful struggle which the nation has maintained for nearly four years, after all the precious blood which has been shed in a war with rebellion, are the rebels to be let off scot-free, and have all they presumptuously ask? Are they to share the fame of revolutionary patriots? Is the rebellion to be christened a Revolution? No, the government is about to do no such weak, mean, wicked thing. With God's help it will crush this unholy rebellion and stamp it with infamy. It will teach ambitious aspirants to irresponsible power, and rebels against the most just and beneficent government in the world a lesson which will humble them for life.

The masses, who are victims rather than responsible agents, should receive clemency, but the originators and leaders of the stupendous crime should be visited with such condign punishment as will be a terror to traitors for all time to come. In justice they should be hung, shot, or banished, under military law, as soon as they are caught. God has spoken no peace for them, nor has he spoken a peace which would give them the opportunity to repeat their treason.

[The preceding portion of this discourse was written before the result of the recent conversation between the President and the Secretary of State, and the so-called peace commissioners of the rebels, in Hampton Roads, was known.* Now the philosophy of this peace movement contained in the preceding thoughts is history, and what sensible, unprejudiced man, under the circumstances, regrets the result?

The firmness with which the President adhered to his often-declared principles, granting no peace to rebels without submission to the government as a preliminary condition, meets with the approval of

* This Conference occurred in February, 1865.

the country, and adds to his high reputation for unflinching patriotism. Indeed it is a sublime spectacle to see ABRAHAM LINCOLN, stanch and honest, thus standing resolutely upon the only sure foundation. It seems now to be finally settled that peace, when it comes, will be brought about by successful war. A sad conclusion this, but the only one left to the country. Let prayer be offered up incessantly, that God in his mercy may command the turbulent waves of rebellion to cease, and that we may soon enjoy an honorable, a just, and a lasting peace.]

XIII.

HARDER BLOWS, AND MORE OF THEM.

AND HE SMOTE THRICE, AND STAYED.—2 Kings xiii, 18.

We are now called to contemplate the conduct of a king in the presence of the aged prophet Elisha. The faithful old servant, who had led a life of singular devotion to the interests of religion and of the kingdom of Israel, who had been greatly honored of God with influence over royalty and with miraculous gifts, "was fallen sick of his sickness whereof he died." The kingdom of Israel being greatly harassed by the Syrians, Joash the king visited the holy seer in his sick chamber, not only out of respect for him, but to obtain some of the last rays of prophetic light touching the kingdom. The meeting was affecting. The king wept over the prophet, using the same significant language in relation to Elisha that the prophet had used in relation to Elijah when he was taken up to heaven in a chariot of fire: "My father, my father, the chariot of Israel and the horsemen thereof;" intimating that he was the strength and defense of the state, as well as the great prompter and example of purity and progress to the ancient Church of God. The holy man had been faithful and honored for a long lifetime. His last act was to give lessons to the king, which ought to have prepared him better to meet his high responsibilities.

The instructions, as was common with the old Jewish prophets, were communicated through symbols. The first lesson was given by directing the king to take a bow and arrows, and to shoot from the window eastward, the venerable man putting his hands upon the king's hands. The prophet then indicated the import of the act by the words, "The arrow of the Lord's deliverance, and the arrow of deliverance from Syria;" and then predicted the discomfiture of the Syrians. He then commands the king to take the arrows and "smite upon the ground, and he smote thrice, and stayed. And the man of God was wroth with him, and said, Thou shouldest have smitten five or six times; then hadst thou smitten Syria till thou hadst consumed it."

The prophet's object was to test the moral qualities of his royal visitor, and to give such instructions as the occasion might require.

By the symbolical act which he dictated, he brought out the king's insight into the facts and circumstances by which he was surrounded, the strength and scope of his desires and purposes, and his faith in God. A man's zeal and strength of heart, and his general qualifications for a great movement, will be indicated by the tone of his conduct in general, and by the smallest preparatory arrangements.

His muscular motions, his step, his mien, his eye, his whole bearing show the qualities of the soul he has in him, and lay a foundation for hope or despair in relation to his course of life or any great undertaking. The king "smote thrice, and stayed. And the man of God was wroth."

Why was the prophet displeased? The king showed himself a dull scholar. He should have known that his actions were to indicate his qualifications for the emergencies before him, and his success in the struggle in which he was about to engage. The prophet's explanation of the shooting from the window ought to have taught him so much as this. He should have known that the nerve he exhibited upon the occasion would be a foreshadowing of the character of his future administration and the measure of its success. In the first instance the old prophet summoned up all his remaining strength, and put his hands upon the king's hands and drew up the arrow to the very head, that it might fly far and indicate a mighty victory. The prophet's hand was in the matter and the work was well done. When the king was directed to strike upon the ground, without the prophet's interference, if he had been broad awake he would have said to himself, "Now I am to show how my work will be done when the old seer is no more and I am left to act alone. I must now smite many times and with all my might, or it will be evident enough that I shall make a failure." He had not, however, taken in the lesson; he exhibited lamentable dullness. The manner of his performing the act seemed to say, "What is the use of all this? The thing is unmeaning. The prophet was once wise, but now he is old and foolish. I will do as directed to satisfy the old man, but it means nothing and will amount to nothing."

Great dullness and little progress under the best teachers, and with the best opportunities, are enough to kindle the ire of the wise and the good. The slothful and the indolent derive little improvement from all the lessons of wisdom lavished upon them. They "are ever learning and never coming to the knowledge of the truth."

The king manifested little earnestness of spirit. Coldness, slowness of motion, weakness of purpose, feebleness and indecision, are great defects in a ruler, and are not compatible with great moral breadth and strength in any one. It is an occasion of grief to the wise and good to see a man in an elevated and a responsible position deficient in motive power, moving with hesitation, and devising half-way measures. Such give little promise of success, and are not candidates for honorable distinction. Be he a civil or military officer, a representative in the legislature or a minister of the Gospel, he will be an occasion of disappointment and mortification to his friends; but this is not all the evil which will follow. Great public interests will be put at hazard, and will probably suffer serious damage. Those who may have an interest in the reputation of the actor, and those who may feel a concern for the interest committed to his hands, will naturally be unpleasantly affected by the failure of the delinquent party. The prophet was angry on both of these accounts. He saw the king was not adequate to his position, and was likely to suffer the disgrace of failure, and then he saw a still more fearful evil in the sufferings which would come upon his people, and the disgrace which the nation would suffer.

The want of nerve in a public functionary is a great disgrace to him, and often a great public calamity. An irresolute, a weak, or a lukewarm officer of the civil government, or of the army, may be an occasion of great disaster.

The want of spirit in any one is a melancholy instance of shortcoming and a certain precursor of defeat. The young aspirant for fame or usefulness bids fair to succeed or fail, according to the earnestness or half-heartedness with which he enters upon life's great work. If he makes a bold strike and pushes out his plans with energy he will probably succeed; but if he is not more than half-resolved and prosecutes his schemes feebly, he is sure to fail. Energy, confidence in himself, and decided measures, are indispensable prerequisites to a history that shall be honorable to himself and beneficial to the world.

What perfect contrasts to the character of King

Joash were Alexander, Oliver Cromwell, Napoleon Bonaparte, George Washington, Lord Chatham, Martin Luther, John Calvin, James Arminius, John Wesley, and Francis Asbury! How largely decision, promptness, and energy entered into the composition of these historical characters need not be proved by particular facts. Their whole lives were made up of a continued series of earnest and decided efforts to achieve great ends. In them there was no weakness of purpose, no hesitation, no tardiness, no dozing over great schemes, no delaying until the main chance was lost; but *action* was their motto, timely action, prompt action, energetic action, persevering action. One of them, the great Napoleon, was accustomed to say that he considered nothing done while anything remained to be done.

There was evident in King Joash a great want of faith. Had the king been in possession of a strong faith he would have appreciated the act dictated by the prophet. A strong faith is of quick discernment. It sees the hand of God in everything, and it puts importance upon the smallest things which are matters of divine direction. It presumes that there is wisdom in what seems unmeaning, if it be a divine requirement. It presumes all to be right and wise which God does or requires, and acts in accordance with that presumption. King Joash, in this case, seemed to look no further than the mere appearance of a small and simple act which, according to the conclusions of human reason, was of no significance; whereas, had his faith been active, he would have said, " This thing is of God, and cannot but be full of meaning. There must be something in it of interest to the kingdom, and of course.of interest to me also." Such a faith would have been an inspiration; would have assured him of something sublime and glorious connected with the simple act of striking the ground with the arrows.

> "The things unknown to feeble sense,
> Unseen by reason's glimmering ray,
> With strong commanding evidence,
> Their heavenly origin display."

Faith not only is eagle-eyed to see God in his word and in his works, but it begets action. It is a fire in the soul, a mighty motive-power. One who is under its inspiration will act with decision and strength. With him what is worth doing at all is worth doing well. He resolves, and proceeds immediately to act, and he acts with heart. His soul is in whatever he does. Faith produces works, and works are the evidence of faith. " By works is faith made perfect." Had the old king possessed the true faith, and possessed it in sufficient amount, he would have smitten the ground until he had beaten the arrows to splinters; he would with them have jarred the earth and raised a cloud of dust. There would have been work there and a mighty clatter which would in some measure have represented the noise of the battle, and a breaking to pieces of the old Syrian empire. But being "of little faith," "he struck thrice, and stayed.". The old prophet was "wroth." The Hebrew root נָצַח signifies *to cut up, to break in pieces.** The man of God was "cut up." His feelings were lacerated; he was wounded and grieved at the king's shortcomings, and the consequences which he foresaw.

Let us now proceed to apply the principles above brought out to our own time, and the circumstances by which we are surrounded.

The rebellion against the government has assumed a magnitude which requires vast outlays of men and money. Half measures but aggravate the evil. Our disasters, in all cases, have resulted from insufficient forces, or a want of understanding the magnitude of the emergency. We want no more long pauses for want of men; we are weary with being met by "a superior force." Let us now give the War Department all the men which its necessities require. Parsimony is often waste; it is especially so in this case. The more valiant soldiers we have in the field the less liable we are to lose them. Liberality in the supply is economy of life. Increase the army to the requisite strength and blood will cease to flow, and the war of the rebellion will soon be brought to a close. Let the *three hundred thousand* men called for by the President be forthcoming, and Jefferson Davis will soon enjoy the luxury of losing his precious life

* See Gesenius's Hebrew Lexicon.

in his experiment of a southern confederacy. The government has a true appreciation of the magnitude of the work on hand, and is now laboring hard to bring the supply up fully to the measure of the demand. The legislative and the executive departments of the government are both straining every nerve to meet the necessities of the hour, and nothing should be in the way.

There is in many quarters a mortal horror of "the draft," and cowards and secession sympathizers vie with each other in their efforts to avoid it. Some run, some hide, and others risk their necks in various ways to avoid being shot on the battle-field. This is all wrong, shameful. He who is not willing to fight for his country ought not to have a country; and he who would sacrifice the life of his country to save his own places a higher estimate upon his life than any one else does; and while he considers himself as outweighing the country that gives him protection, it is probable that history will not consider his name worthy of a record. As to those citizens of foreign birth who have come to our country to escape from oppression and to secure the means of a comfortable living, and have exercised the right of voting at the polls, who run away and leave their wives and children to work for themselves, especially young men of this class who have no families to provide for, language furnishes no terms to express the contempt in which they ought to be held. As the draft is the only method by which the army can be reinforced with sufficient dispatch to meet the emergencies of the country, it is unpatriotic either to oppose or to embarrass it. The necessities of the country have demanded large contributions of men and money, and the same necessities remain. Why withhold now when the national arms are everywhere successful, and only another campaign, well sustained by recruits, and ably managed, as it will no doubt be by our great army and naval commanders, will suffice to bring the rebellion to a close.

It would undoubtedly be preferable to replenish the army by enlistments if the thing were feasible; but the demand is urgent; *time* is everything in a campaign. There must be no delay; there can be none without peril to the country's cause. A large reinforcement of the army is absolutely necessary, and if the necessity is not met by volunteering, the government must resort to compulsion; and what plan could be devised more equitable to decide the question as to who shall go into the service than by lot? If a draft must be made, then all must be drafted, or a part. If only a part of the able-bodied men subject to military duty are needed, how shall the question be settled, who the fortunate men shall be who shall have the honor of periling their lives for their country, if not by the method which the government has adopted, and which meets with the approval of all civilized nations? Jefferson Davis conscripts all, from sixteen to fifty-five; we only take one sixth, from twenty-one to forty-five. Surely if it is a hardship to be a patriot, it is a much greater hardship to be a rebel; and if the people of the rebellious states submit to a merciless, indiscriminate conscription of all who have physical strength to carry a gun, surely we ought not to complain if the government, in an equitable way, selects a portion of such as are capable of military duty to meet the exigencies of this great war. Come on, fellow-citizens, there is no time for paltering; now is the time to strike; heavy blows now will do the work.

Again, let it be observed that the demand of the times upon our army and navy is for great skill and great bravery. The cause of the country, thank God, is not likely to suffer from a deficiency in the leadership. At present we have at the head of the army one whom Providence seems to have raised up for the emergency, and he is sustained by officers little inferior to himself. While Grant, Sherman, Thomas, and Sheridan are in the field, and Farragut and Porter are leading on the navy, we have little more to desire in the way of leadership. Many other names are entitled to be placed in the category of meritorious and distinguished officers who have the full confidence of the country, and have already won for themselves a name in history. With such leaders at the head of our brave boys we do not anticipate a failure. Failure there cannot be with such a cause as we have; but we want early success, complete success, success with as little loss as possible in overthrowing the rebellion.

The spirit of the army and navy is good, the bravery of our troops is without a parallel, our commanders were never excelled in the annals of war; and now what is wanted is heavy blows and a great many of them, and this is what we shall have. We want such blows as were struck at Fort Donelson, at New Orleans, at Vicksburg, in Georgia, at Nashville, in the Shenandoah, and at Fort Fisher. Such blows we want struck at Mobile, at Charleston, and at Richmond. At the last-named place we hope ere long to see the finishing stroke given.

The present crisis calls for *harder blows, and more of them.* Let this be our motto. We want substantial victories, not such as the rebels have had hundreds of. They report their victories dayly, but through some mysterious cause they are all "without results;" they are either just where they were before, or "a little back of their old lines." Nor do we want such victories as several which we have had on our side. Such, for instance, as those of "the seven days' fight" down from Richmond, when, although the general in command whipped Lee and Jackson every day, he "fell back every night" to find "a more advantageous base."

Indeed, we want something a little different from

the victories of Antietam and Gettysburgh. There "they smote thrice and stayed." The rebels were whipped, but got away; they should have been "smitten until they were consumed." Following up one blow with another in quick succession is the secret of telling victories. This striking and then *staying* is not the thing; we want more *unconditional surrenders.* That must be the watchword at Wilmington, at Mobile, at Charleston, and at Richmond. Hannibal, one of the greatest captains of ancient story, crossed the Alps with a vast army of his Carthaginians and beat the Romans in four great battles. The last of the four was that of Cannæ, upon which the old historian, Collier, remarks: "A prodigious victory, the consequences whereof must have been the ruin and downfall of the Roman commonwealth had Hannibal known how to use it; but instead of going straight to Rome he went to Capua, where he wintered, and the delights of the place debauched his whole army, while the Romans recovered themselves." The result of this relaxation of his zeal, of staying his hands, was his retreat from Italy and the destruction of Carthage.

It has not been the method of Grant, Sherman, and Thomas to strike thrice and then stay, and, after the example of the Carthaginian general, allow their troops to indulge in ease and luxuries until they become demoralized, and the rebels have time to recover their strength and begin another campaign with invigorated and largely increased forces. Grant is holding Lee's great army at Richmond, Sherman is moving upon Charleston, and Thomas upon Mobile. These winter campaigns in the South and Southwest bid fair to terminate the rebellion in that direction within the next few months, so we now hope and believe.

The enemy must have no time to rest and recuperate. The pursuit must be ardent and close; blow must follow blow in quick succession. Let the tread of our cavalry, the huzzas of our brave boys, and the thunder of our cannon, haunt the rebel armies day and night, and hurry them from one retreat to another, until they are captured, surrender, or are "consumed." Now, brave fellows,

"Strike!
Strike for your altars and your fires!
God and your native land."

XIV.

THE SECESSION DEVIL.

THIS KIND GOETH NOT OUT BUT BY PRAYER AND FASTING.
Matt. xvii, 21.

THE existence of invisible, malignant beings, who exercise an injurious influence over the moral character and happiness of mankind, is directly or indirectly acknowledged by all religions. It is also as generally presumed that it is the work of religion to counteract this influence. The appropriate and effective provisions for the accomplishment of this great and good object are, however, only to be found in Christianity.

It seems that demons were permitted anciently to exercise an influence over the bodies of men, though this power, since the general spread of the Gospel, has been restrained. As to the particular reasons for the difference in this respect I shall not at present be curious to inquire. But that the demoniacal possessions of which we have so many accounts in the New Testament history were realities, and not, as some insist, mere diseases, is evident from the fact that these demons often conversed and reasoned, desired and feared. These acts could scarcely be attributed to diseases in the most impassioned poetry; but to introduce them into sober narrative would be an absurdity that would hardly find a parallel.

Several of the fathers supposed that the word γενος, *kind*, referred to the whole genus of devils. The same view is taken of the subject by Dr. S. Clarke among the older, and by Dr. Bloomfield among the recent English commentators. Others, as Doddridge, Coke, and Benson, suppose that this hypothesis does not account for the disappointment of the apostles in not being able to eject this devil, nor for the answer given by our Lord to their inquiry. Why some devils should be more obstinate and difficult to eject than others is not easy to perceive; and yet there is nothing in the *fact* any more inconsistent with reason than that these malignant powers should at all commune with the minds of men and exercise an influence over them.

"This demon," says Dr. A. Clarke, "may be considered an *emblem of deeply rooted vices and inveterate habits*, over which the conquest is not generally obtained but through extraordinary humiliations." This is a practical view of the subject which is both reasonable and safe. He who would root out cherished lusts and long-established habits undertakes no ordinary work, and stands in need of more than ordinary preparation.

What are the evils which we as a nation most severely suffer from at the present?

Is there not a fearful amount of *ignorance* among

the great mass of our population? I mean not merely ignorance of the arts and sciences, for this species of ignorance sometimes consists with a high degree of moral worth; but more especially ignorance of the great principles and requirements of religion, and of the duties, responsibilities, rights, and privileges of citizens. These two branches of this deadly upas always unite in the same trunk, and are always, so far as they exert an influence, destructive of the best interests of society. But we not only have an abundance of this evil among us which is of native growth, but vast masses of it are constantly drifting upon our shores from the old world, and the whole combining lies like an incubus upon the very vitals of the body politic. Our institutions cannot be preserved in safety and prosperity by ignorance. They are, indeed, eminently imperiled by the prevalence of this curse of the human soul, and especially so when it is united with a superstitious veneration for corrupt forms of religion and implicit obedience to a designing priesthood. And who does not see that there is enough of this deadly leaven in our country to work our ruin unless by some efficient remedy it shall speedily be neutralized?

Is not *infidelity* sadly prevalent in our country? This evil takes various hues, according to its various associations. We sometimes see it assume the garb of philosophy, at other times that of politics, and still at others that of the most degrading vice. Philosophical infidelity is reason run mad; political infidelity is liberty without restraint; and vulgar infidelity is a full license of the grosser passions. Whatever its form, it is the same enemy to the improvement and happiness of man. A nation of infidels could not long exist. It would very soon burst like a bubble, and be numbered among the things that *were*. And this obstinate demon is lurking about in all directions; and though he may cover himself with the garb of religion, he is no less a devil at heart, nor any less dangerous to the public weal. I need not tell you that this malignant spirit has shown himself in the high places of power as well as in the haunts of vice and dissipation; that he has his trained bands firmly organized and regularly disciplined; that he has seized upon the press, and has flooded the country with books, pamphlets, and periodicals, containing the most alarming developments of his real malignity; that he has turned tract distributer, missionary, prophet, and what not; that he has actually compassed sea and land to make proselytes. All this is perfectly notorious. At present the monster seems to have secreted himself; but he is still alive, and only waits a fair opportunity to make new demonstrations of his utter hostility, not only to Christianity, but to the very existence of the social compact.

Does not *pride* exist to an alarming extent among us? We need not attempt to trace out and identify this evil in all its various forms. It will be sufficient to notice it as it influences individuals, as it affects the national character, and as it shows itself in our religion. We may call individual pride decency and self-respect, national pride a patriotic concern for the nation's honor, and religious pride a pious regard to the decencies of divine institutions; but it is still the same accursed thing, which the Lord abhors. And where are the footsteps of this rebellious demon not seen? I need not point you to his infallible tokens; they are everywhere displayed before the gaze of earth and heaven.

Nor should it be necessary to premonish you of its ruinous consequences. The word of God and the pages of history are replete with instructions upon the subject. History, it is said, is philosophy teaching by example. Let us, then, through this medium look at Nineveh, Babylon, Tyre, Greece, and Rome, and learn that "he who exalteth himself shall be abased;" that "pride goeth before destruction, and a haughty spirit before a fall." Let us mark the fate of Sennacherib, of Nebuchadnezzar, and of Herod, and remember that the same God who in these instances eminently punished pride, still reigns, and has the same abhorrence of this accursed principle.

Is not *selfishness* a ruling principle among us! By selfishness I do not mean a due regard to our own best interests: this is so far from being wrong that it is enforced by the obligations of religion. But I refer to private ends arrayed against the general good. And how has this principle shown itself, not only in the various departments of business, and in political maneuvers, but even in our benevolent enterprises! How common is it, when a politician becomes extremely jealous of the liberties of the country and of the rights of his fellow-citizens, for him to be suspected of some little regard to the loaves and fishes of office! And is not this suspicion founded on a numerous class of facts, which give but too strong ground for a correct induction? Witness the violations of public confidence upon the part of this class of men, and especially the *peculations* and *defalcations* of public functionaries, which are by no means strange events.

I have noticed but a small portion of this species of evil. We cannot go into detail without becoming lost in the maze. Who can look away from dear self and seek the good of the whole, losing his own interest in the general welfare? Such individuals, thank God, there are; but certainly they are quite too rare for the honor and prosperity of our beloved country.

Is not *avarice* a prevailing vice in this land? This is a species under the genus selfishness; but it figures so largely as to require separate notice. What an excitement! what a stir! what a rage does this miserable demon constantly keep up! Is it any wonder that intelligent travelers suppose mammon to be the god of the Americans? M. de Tocqueville, an intelligent Frenchman, says:

"A native of the United States clings to this world's goods as if he were certain never to die; and he is so hasty at grasping at all within his reach, that one would suppose he was constantly afraid of not living long enough to enjoy them. He clutches everything, he holds nothing fast, but soon loosens his grasp to pursue fresh gratifications. A man builds a house to spend his later years in, and sells it before the roof is on: he plants a garden, and lets it just as the trees are coming into bearing: he brings a field into tillage, and leaves other men to gather the crops: he embraces a profession, and gives it up: he settles in a place which he soon after leaves to carry his changeable longings elsewhere. If his private affairs leave him any leisure, he instantly plunges into the vortex of politics: and if at the end of a year of unremitting labor he finds he has a few days' vacation, his eager curiosity whirls him over the vast extent of the United States, and he will travel fifteen hundred miles in a few days to shake off his happiness. Death at length overtakes him, but it is before he is weary of his bootless chase of that complete felicity which is ever on the wing." All we can say to this is, that it is but too true a picture of what is every day passing before our eyes.

All these are personal sins which involve personal guilt, but they may become so general as to bring down the vengeance of God upon the whole land. In addition to those individual delinquencies, we have great national sins, for which God holds us accountable as a nation; and as nations, as such, cannot be punished in the world to come, we are fearfully amenable to national judgments, which are the ordinary means by which national offenses are punished.

I am not aware that, as a nation, we have been guilty of the violation of national law to the injury of weaker powers. Although we have no occasion for humiliation on this account, we have occasion for deep repentance on account of wrongs done to classes of men over whose destiny we have had absolute control.

The first instance of national sin which I notice here is gross injustice to the aborigines of this country. The poor natives of the soil have been driven from their homes and the graves of their fathers, and one compulsory remove after another, westward, has brought them into many sad extremities, and to the very verge of despair. The government has not always kept the faith of treaties with these poor savages. Too often have voracious land-pirates and unscrupulous state authorities found the means of using the United States government as a tool for the achievement of stupendous robberies inflicted upon the native tribes. As a nation we have to plead guilty to this fearful indictment, and throw ourselves upon the mercy of the court of heaven. Under later administrations the government has been exerting itself commendably to make amends for former errors, and has, to a great extent, regained the confidence of the Indian tribes nearest to the borders of civilization. Still it would not be wise in us to ignore the fact of former wrongs.

Another instance of national transgression is that of the enslavement of the African race. It is true, that African slavery had its origin, in this country, before our existence as an independent nation commenced; that African slavery was an inheritance left to us by the mother country. We, however, have fearful responsibilities in the matter. Although fenced in by state rights, the whole country has been involved in the responsibility in various ways. The institution of slavery has been our great national sin, and our greatest disgrace. This sin has brought upon us the judgments of God with almost crushing weight.

Thank God, this national crime and national curse is about to be wiped out. President Lincoln's proclamation, emancipating all the slaves in the rebellious states, and the passage of the amendment to the Constitution, by a two thirds vote of both houses of Congress, prohibiting slavery, or involuntary servitude, except for crime, throughout the United States, have relieved the general government of all further responsibility in the matter. Now, if a majority of three fourths of the legislatures of the several states pass the amendment, slavery ceases to exist in the United States. It is devoutly to be hoped that the requisite majority of the state legislatures will do themselves the credit to pass the amendment and so end the accursed institution of slavery in the country. If the amendment should not obtain the sanction of the states, the guilt of the institution will no longer be national, but will rest upon the heads of the delinquent states.

There is one monster devil with which the nation is tortured which must be placed prominently as *the great evil* of these times. This is the SECESSION DEVIL.

Other evil spirits give us great trouble, but this one the most of all, because he is the most obstinate, the most malignant, and the most destructive of them all.

The *secession devil* is a *rebellious* devil.

He rebels against law and order, against laws which God has ordained, laws which the people have enacted, and laws which he has sworn to keep. He despises the Constitution, tramples upon the Declaration of Independence, and sets at naught all legitimate authority, human and divine.

He is an *ambitious* devil.

He is, I suspect, that very devil whom Milton reports to have said that he "had rather reign in hell than serve in heaven." He seeks dominion, he loves the highest places, he aspires to absolute power. He says, "If he had a thousand lives he would sacrifice them all rather than not establish his rebel kingdom."

He is a *lying* devil.

He carries on his old game of deception. In old times he tempted mother Eve with the forbidden fruit, and said, "Ye shall not surely die," but eat the fruit and "ye shall be as gods." So still he deceives the people with his lies. He tells them that secession is right, is wise, and that if they hold out a little longer England and France will acknowledge their independence, and the federal government will acknowledge it too. He tells them that he has the best of it in every battle, and what he loses is not worth having. These and a thousand other lies he thrusts down the throats of his vassals, and some of them think it all true as preaching.

He is a *thieving* devil.

He stole the government property. He plunders the people, even his own dear subjects, and tells them to charge all to the necessities of the state; he steals cotton to pay his confederate loan; in fact, lays his hands on whatever he wants, no matter whose it is, or however needy its owner.

He is a *cruel* devil.

His heartless cruelty is seen in the blood he has caused to be shed for the establishment of his slave confederacy, in the widows and orphans he has made, the hearths he has desolated, the broken hearts, the tears and sighs which he has occasioned for a bauble. In old times this devil had great power over his subjects, and inflicted upon them great tortures. He threw them down; they cried out, they were convulsed, they foamed, they wallowed in the dirt. The torments which he inflicts upon those whom he possesses now are not inferior to those which he inflicted then. If ever there was a people "scattered and peeled," plundered, whipped, thrown down, and rolled in the mud, bedraggled, booted, and skinned, they are the victims of secession.

He is a *mean* devil.

Of old he entered into the *swine;* now he inhabits *guerrillas*, his tenements growing more and more despicable. He repudiates his bonds, robs the poor to feed his soldiers, and deals in contemptible arts to keep up a show of nobility.

Finally, he is a *religious* devil.

This strange devil prays and fasts and keeps thanksgivings. In the days of Christ this same evil spirit exhibited his proclivities in the Pharisees, "making long prayers at the corners of the streets," and fasting, to be seen of men. Now he prays for the triumph of the rebellion, and for the destruction of the Union troops and the Union cause.

These *pious devils* are the worst that ever came to this poor unfortunate world. They have a *conscience*, and who dare oppose the dictates of conscience? They talk of the obligations of religion, and in the sacred name of religion they break every precept of the decalogue. See how pious these rebels are. Surely, says the simple dupe, God must be on their side. The devil prayed to Christ, saying, "Let us alone;

why art thou come to torment us before the time?" The secession demon makes the same prayer to the Yankee government: "Let us alone; why are you come to trouble us? I adjure you by God that ye torment me not." All in character, praying and swearing mixed together.

We have now noticed "seven abominations," as many as there were devils in Mary Magdalene, which more or less involve the national character. The whole together may be "called legion, for they are many;" and they are most *obstinate* and *inveterate* in their character. They are *strongly posted*, and will never yield to mild measures. He who would eradicate any one of them must gird himself for a strong effort, and certainly if we would engage them all we need most solemn preparation.

We come to inquire into the means by which these evils may be successfully encountered.

But before we enter upon the discussion of the true remedy, let us glance at sundry unauthorized means which are often resorted to for the cure of national evils.

Political changes are often relied upon. Were we to believe our pseudo-patriots, we might expect that a change in the administration of the government would sweep all the disorders of the land, moral, political, and physical, into eternal annihilation. If we only mind them, they would fain have us expect for ourselves and our children, health, peace, wealth, and happiness forever. But though such changes might be really important, they by no means reach the foundations and sources of the mischief. The evils are of a *moral* character, and will yield only to moral remedies.

This, however, is not the course taken by blind zealots. They fall upon those they deem in error with hard names and abusive epithets, and think thus to drive the devil out of them. But their course and their success are very much like those of "certain vagabond Jews" who attempted to imitate the apostles in the exercise of their miraculous powers. "They took upon them to call over them which had evil spirits the name of the Lord Jesus, saying, We adjure you by Jesus, whom Paul preacheth." But "the evil spirit answered and said, Jesus I know, and Paul I know; but who are ye? And the man in whom the evil spirit was, leaped on them, and overcame them, so that they fled out of that house naked and wounded." Now upon this instructive piece of history we may observe, *first*, that they proceeded without any authority; and, *secondly*, the result was that the devil triumphed, and they were most miserably disgraced.

But men may really have a good end in view, and may be influenced by an ardent zeal, and yet only prejudice the cause by the manner in which they undertake to accomplish it. In all cases when self-styled reformers undertake to remedy evils in their own strength, and by their own wisdom, the devil is more than a match for them. He falls upon *them* without giving up his *prey*, and so the evil is aggravated in the subject, and reacts upon the self-prompted instrument of deliverance.

How much of empiricism is there in religion and politics! For reigning evils there are many nostrums prescribed. The press teems with infallible cures for all the disorders of the times; but how many patients die under the treatment of empirics perhaps will only be known in the great day of final reckoning. They promise us long life and good days; but let us beware, there may be "death in the pot." All these experiments are as unnecessary as they are dangerous, for a remedy, a sovereign remedy, is at hand.

The only remedy for the disorders of the human heart is the abounding grace of God, through Jesus Christ. The means then by which this grace is obtained and made to bear directly upon the disease is the matter of inquiry.

The leading condition is an *operative faith*.

Our Saviour tells the disciples that the reason they could not eject the devil, in the case delineated, was "because of their unbelief;" and then proceeds to say, "Verily I say unto you, If ye have faith as a grain of mustard seed, ye shall say unto this mountain, Remove hence to yonder place; and it shall remove; and nothing shall be impossible unto you."

It is probable our Lord here refers primarily to *the faith of miracles*, the smallest amount of which should be sufficient to remove the greatest obstacles. But in a more general application of the text, "faith as a grain of mustard seed" may, as Dr. Clarke says, import "a growing, active faith."

The faith of the Church is the great conservative principle, upon which depend the hopes and happiness of a lost world. I speak not now of the faith of miracles. This, for wise reasons, long since ceased from the Church. I speak of that vital energy which gives efficiency to the instituted means of grace, and arms the Church against the charms of the world and the powers of hell. Its essential principles are a conviction of the truth of the Gospel, a submission to the terms of salvation, and a trust in the promises of God. This faith fails not to regulate both the heart and life, and to give effect to all God's appointed means for the melioration of human condition.

The great apostle of the Gentiles, in the eleventh chapter of the Epistle to the Hebrews, pronounces the greatest eulogium upon this faith that can be conceived, by simply giving us a view of some of its achievements. He defines it in the outset by giving us a view of its practical workings. "Now," says he, "faith is the substance of things hoped for, the evidence of things not seen." He then proceeds to set before us an array of the most sublime examples of it recorded in the sacred story. In these we have practical demonstrations of the power and efficacy of this great leading principle of Christianity.

Nor is this faith any less necessary for us than it was for the patriarchs, prophets, and apostles of olden time. We can neither do anything toward working out our own salvation, or helping to reclaim others, without the constant action of a vital faith. Without this our arm will be nerveless and all our efforts fruitless. The devil will withstand us at every point and foil us in every struggle. And how will go the war that the American Church has waged against the numerous forms of vice which are prevalent in our land, unless she is deeply imbued with faith? Alas, she will come out of the battle " naked and wounded," and hell will hold a day of rejoicing. Hear the blessed Saviour say, " Have faith in God." Hear him expostulating with us, " Why is it that ye have no faith?" "Why are ye fearful, O ye of little faith?" In a conflict with the devil all human power is mocked, and reason utterly confounded. How will the Church " wrestle against flesh and blood and principalities and powers, and against spiritual wickedness in high places," without a strong hold upon " the mighty God of Jacob?" Truly this is her only hope!

The next condition necessary to secure divine help is *prayer*.

Prayer is the offering up of the desires of the heart

to God; it is the soul's converse with the Invisible; and it is acceptable only when associated with the faith of which we have spoken. A mere form of words, without any corresponding emotions and affections, is nothing worth. Prayer is begging, and hence the spirit, the language, and the posture should all be appropriate. Where would be the fitness in a poor miserable beggar coming to your door with a great parade of ceremonies, or a mere form of words? Would it not rather be expected that his expressions, his attitude, his sighs, his tears, his broken utterance, would go to enforce his application? I say nothing against appropriate forms of prayer to be used upon certain occasions, much less would I give place to an incoherent manner of expression; but I would have all the members of the Church so many officiating priests, offering up to God the sacrifice of pure devotion, *according to their several ability*. I would have the thoughts, the desires, and the words of the whole Church combined and mingled in a common offering to Almighty God. I would have every one bring his own offering, be it ever so small, and cast it into God's treasury, until the grand aggregate shall constitute a unanimous expression, and go up to God like the sound of many waters, and be an odor of sweet smell unto our heavenly Father.

To prayer belong petition, deprecation, intercession, and thanksgiving. We ask for blessings for ourselves; we deprecate the divine displeasure; we bring our brethren of the human race in the arms of our charity, and ask God to bless and save them; and finally we render thanks to Almighty God for what he has done for us and them. The duty must be performed in public, in the domestic circle, and in the closet. But its acceptableness depends entirely upon the spirit and temper of mind in which it is performed. I have already suggested that it must be offered in *faith*. To this quality must be added humility, fervor or earnestness, and perseverance. As we have always the same need of prayer, we must "pray without ceasing," "pray always, and not faint." As it is the language of dependence, of poverty, and want, it is never out of time. Indeed, the Christian's very breath should be prayer. His aspirations, warm from his heart, should come up before God like the morning sacrifice, every hour. He should cultivate a habitual sense of his dependence on God, devotion should constitute his prevailing mental state, and his whole life should be one unbroken series of heavenly aspirations.

And if the Church were brought up to this state, what efficiency would she possess, what power with God, what triumph over sin, what burning charity, what a halo of glory would surround her!

To faith and prayer we must add *fasting*.

Upon the duty of fasting we shall first make a few general remarks, and then proceed to consider it in relation to present circumstances.

This duty is united with faith and prayer. "Thence learn," says Burkitt, "that fasting and prayer are two special means of Christ's appointment for the enabling us victoriously to overcome Satan, and to cast him out of ourselves and others. We must set an edge upon our faith by prayer, and upon our prayer by fasting."

Christian fasting is a temporary abstinence from food; neither so excessive as to produce exhaustion, nor yet so partial as to produce no sensible effect upon the physical and mental frame. This duty, accompanied by humble prayer and an obedient faith, humbles and subdues the heart. There is a constant tendency in our animal appetites to triumph over reason and conscience. A perpetual effort is necessary to enable the moral and the rational part to overcome the animal. By mortifying and subduing the flesh, and by cherishing the intellectual and moral man, we become prepared for strong intellectual and moral efforts. But fasting is a divine institution, and its utility does not depend upon its natural effects upon the body or the mind so much as upon the blessing of God. For God will always visit with special favor acts of obedience performed *because* he requires them, and is glorified in them. Our true attitude is that of submission; and even where we can see no special adaptedness in the duty required to promote good, still for us "obedience is better than sacrifice, and to hearken than the fat of rams." God has the undoubted right to connect antecedent and sequence as he sees best; and when the fact of such connection is revealed, it does not become us to refuse obedience because we cannot perceive the reasons for such connection. So if God require us to fast he will bless us in so doing. This we might infer from the character of God, if we had no facts upon record which bear upon the point. But while we have before us the instructive examples of Daniel, of Esther, and of the Ninevites; of Moses, of John the Baptist, and of Christ himself, there is left no room for question as to the acceptableness and the efficacy of fasting rightly performed.

Fasting is one of the Christian duties that are not to be confined to days set apart by the civil authorities, but is to be resorted to voluntarily at set periods, or upon any great and pressing emergency. I am not now called upon to enforce the due observance of a national fast, but to urge frequent fasting and prayer with reference to our national troubles. The nation is suffering fearfully, and although the principal cause is from a wicked rebellion, there can be no doubt but God has permitted this rebellion for the chastisement of the nation. It then becomes us to fast and pray, and to humble ourselves before God.

The demon of secession, as has been seen, is a most obstinate spirit, and hard to manage. He may be conquered and broken down by physical force, but he cannot be cast out without divine help. His object is the ruin of all that is fair and glorious in our free institutions. Whatever motives we have for the salvation of our beloved country urge us to humble ourselves with prayer and fasting, to deprecate the wrath of heaven, and labor for the removal of the evils brought into the body politic, and those which still threaten to enter through the agency of the *secession devil*.

The battle is of the Lord, hence his aid is to be sought as our only hope. We must have large and well-appointed armies, brave and skillful officers, and our armies must stand up manfully against the foe, while the whole country must *fast and pray*. We must follow the instructions of that brave old warrior Oliver Cromwell: "Boys, pray all the time, but keep your powder dry." God works by authorized means. Having done our best, we may safely commit the cause of the country "to Him who judgeth righteously." I will now close this disquisition by reference to several motives which the Christian citizen has for a large outlay of means for the promotion of the moral improvement of the people and the perpetuity of the union of these United States.

Our *natural self-love* should prompt us to such efforts.

Is the security of life, of property, and of character a matter of importance? Do we instinctively desire it? And shall we have no concern for the safety and permanency of those institutions upon which this security depends? Surely, as we desire our own peace and safety, and the happiness of our children, we can but be disposed to do everything within our power to elevate the moral character of the people in these United States, and to restore law and order. Here the people are the source of all civil power. They have the government in their own hands; and if they become generally corrupt and fail to sustain it, they will soon bring ruin upon themselves. And the righteous will suffer with the wicked. Though there might be multitudes of pious and patriotic individuals, they could have no security or safety in a general wreck of our civil institutions. Anarchy and confusion would inevitably follow the general prevalence of vice and licentiousness, and the overthrow of the Constitution and the laws. Morality and religion constitute the bonds by which society is held together, and without them the elements of the social compact will be dissolved. Inattention to the moral character of the people is recklessness of our own personal safety and prosperity. It is suicide.

Patriotism calls aloud for these efforts. If the prosperity and happiness of our country and the permanency of our free institutions depend upon the *virtue of the people*, and this none will dispute, how can we more directly serve the interests of our beloved country than by seeking to promote her moral improvement? Tyrants know full well that *the suc-*

cess of free institutions in this country is the *doom of despotism* throughout the earth. Of course they watch for our halting. They mark with a kind of diabolical satisfaction the progress of those causes which tend to our ruin. When we stumble, they say, " Aha, so would we have it." Shall their predictions and their wishes be realized in the ultimate dissolution of this purest and best of all human governments? As we love our country, we shall give this interrogation a most *emphatic negative.* And we will sustain our words by appropriate action.

Philanthropy will induce action. As we love our fellow-men, we shall desire the blessings of political freedom to be extended through the world. And when will this be done if the experiment of a popular government in this country prove a failure? When will arbitrary institutions, with all their accompaniments, be annihilated, and *man* be free and happy, if the genius of liberty is driven from our shores? If the war waged by us against rebellion and oppression shall result in defeat, where is the hope of the world?

Finally, *religion* supplies many considerations to urge us to action.

The Church has breasted many storms and triumphed over a multitude of foes. But she has yet a grand, decisive battle to fight here that will tell upon the destinies of the world, and will hold an intimate connection with the glorious millennium. The

American Church will constitute one grand division of the sacramental host in the final struggle with the prince of darkness, and upon her devolves high responsibilities. The manner in which she acts her part is of great importance to the general result.

If Christianity is foiled upon 'American soil, where can she hope for success? Here she stands upon vantage ground. Here she is neither proscribed by the civil power, nor so united to it as to weaken her energies, or deprive her of the glory of her achievements. And shall she prove too feeble for the great work she has undertaken under such favorable circumstances? God forbid! Let her friends rally around her standard and shout for the battle. Let all who love her come up to her help, push on her conquests, *labor, pray, fast, fight*, until her "righteousness shall go forth as brightness, and her salvation as a lamp that burneth;" until rebellion, slavery, and every other form of wickedness shall cease from this renovated and glorious land.

XV.
THE GOOD SAMARITAN.

AND JESUS ANSWERING SAID, A CERTAIN MAN WENT DOWN FROM JERUSALEM TO JERICHO, AND FELL AMONG THIEVES, WHICH STRIPPED HIM OF HIS RAIMENT, AND WOUNDED HIM, AND DEPARTED, LEAVING HIM HALF DEAD. . . . BUT A CERTAIN SAMARITAN, AS HE JOURNEYED, CAME WHERE HE WAS: AND WHEN HE SAW HIM, HE HAD COMPASSION ON HIM, AND WENT TO HIM, AND BOUND UP HIS WOUNDS, POURING IN OIL AND WINE, AND SET HIM ON HIS OWN BEAST, AND BROUGHT HIM TO AN INN, AND TOOK CARE OF HIM.—Luke x, 30, 33-34.

THE story of the wounded Jew and the compassionate Samaritan beautifully illustrates the method of God's providence. It is a law of the divine administration to follow evil with the remedy. The advent of sin, which brought death into the world and all our woe, was followed by the promise of the Saviour, who, in the fullness of time, was manifested in the flesh. He was the world's great Restorer. His grace presented a remedy for the defection of humanity in all its breadth. There is not an attribute or phase of human depravity which has not its counterpart in the Gospel. The doctrines of Christ, each and all, stand in juxtaposition to the various manifestations of human depravity. Where sin has reigned unto death, there grace reigns through righteousness unto eternal life by Jesus Christ our Lord.

The same economy of following the disease by

the remedy is found to characterize God's providential arrangements throughout. Supply follows closely upon the heels of want. The mangled, bleeding victim, cast out and apparently uncared-for, is found by the kind-hearted Samaritan, who binds up his wounds, pouring in oil and wine, and carries him to a place of safety and comfort.

The desolating war in which the country is engaged, to a casual observer, presents a scene of unmitigated horror; but a careful survey of the whole picture will bring out the occasions which it furnishes for the most splendid exhibitions of the better feelings of the human heart, and the divine graces of Christianity.

The war has originated the occasion for two of the noblest institutions which have graced modern civilization: the Sanitary and the Christian Commissions. The first is humanitarian, the second eminently Christian. The first is auxiliary to the commissariat and the medical department, the second is an expansion of the functions of the chaplain; each in its way supplies a desideratum, and, united, they go far toward mitigating the horrors of war. If war can be civilized and Christianized, we have in these institutions the agencies for the accomplishment of these great ends. The wars of the barbarous ages were attended by no such modifying and relieving agencies. Former wars, even of Christian nations, were unattended by the good Samaritan with his oil and wine and ambulance for the relief of those who were weltering in their blood on the gory field of battle.

War seen from afar dazzles the imagination. The mind is filled with emotions of admiration as it contemplates the pomp of martial array, the skill of leaders, the valor of the contending forces, the attack, the thunder of the battle, which shakes the earth and darkens the heavens, the final charge, and the victory, the glad news that thrills along the wires which form the nerves of the nation, the mighty joy which rolls out from the field of strife in an ever-widening circle. But viewed more closely the scene changes; the moral grandeur of the contest may remain, but we learn the fearful price with which victory is bought. We behold the weary march, the crowded hospital, the horrors of the bloody field when the battle is over, and the place of strife is a true Aceldama, where the mangled forms of the living and the dying are sometimes left for days, because, though there are many that pity, there are few that can be spared from the ranks to save them.

In the fearful war which foul rebellion has brought upon the land, our government has done all that lies in its power to alleviate the sufferings of our brave soldiers. Surgeons, hospitals, medical stores, have been provided in abundance. Yet when a great battle occurs, and thousands fall in an hour, some agency is needed to supplement the appliances provided by the public authorities. When a single day's fighting numbers half the officers and men of a regiment among the wounded, the surgeon and his assistant may do all that lies in their power, but many must suffer and die, because there are so many that they cannot all be reached in time. In the permanent hospitals, too, there is work for the humane and the patriotic; a work of benevolence and love, as well as of wisdom, in supplying various comforts and delicacies, which the stern rules of military life never provide, but of which the sick room even of the poor at home is not destitute.

Here, then, is the field of the two Commissions, whose agencies for good the present contest has called into existence. They are the free outgrowth of a nation's grateful regard for its defenders—the voice of peace and good-will heard even amid the lowering storm of war. It is matter of congratulation to note with what liberality the money of the poor and the rich has been contributed, how many willing hands and patriotic hearts have engaged in these blessed ministries of humanity. The Sanitary Commission, from its abundant treasures, the gift of a generous people, has provided the means whereby many a brave man has been saved to the armies of his country, many a husband, a brother, a son, has been preserved to return to the home which mourns his absence; and it has also been laboring with great usefulness and success in behalf of the freedmen of the Mississippi. The Christian Commission, in its proposed department of labor, sweeps a still wider circle. It looks to all the wants of the soldier, physical, mental, and religious, and seeks to do what may be done to provide for them all. It not only has food for the hungry, and clothing for the naked, but sends them by the hands of sympathizing Christian men, who follow the sound of the battle, that they may bear away the wounded and pray beside the dying. At Gettysburgh, before the smoke of the deadly contest had been dispelled, the delegates of the Christian Commission were at their noble toil, which they prosecuted day and night till every bleeding sufferer, patriot or rebel, was found and cared for. The number of delegates thus engaged was over two hundred. Surgeons have declared that, through the agency of the Christian Commission, at least one thousand lives were saved on that field alone. Ministers, who were there engaged in Gospel labors, under the auspices of the Commission, estimate the souls converted in the hospitals at Gettysburgh at one thousand. At this present hour, while the fierce storm of battle rages at various points, hundreds of the delegates of the Commission, a large majority of whom are ministers of the Gospel, are prosecuting their labors among the wounded and the dying, striving with heart and voice to save the lives and souls of those to whom they minister. On every great battle-field, and in every hospital in all the land, their presence has brought comfort and hope; and many a wanderer have they led, through grace, to the fold of Christ. The cash value of the benefactions of the Christian Commission during the past year amounts to nearly a million of dollars, and more than twelve hundred delegates have responded to its call without fee or reward.

"THE CHRISTIAN COMMISSION is a voluntary association. It was organized in New York on the 16th November, 1861. The persons by whom it was organized were delegates from several societies existing in as many cities and other places, known as the Young Men's Christian Associations. The delegates were sent to New York for the purpose of organizing a body to be known as the Christian Commission. The purpose of this body, at the first and at the present, is the performance of such service to the disabled of the Army and Navy as Christian sympathy suggests. In bodies consisting of large numbers of men it is well known that there must be many sick, and in the sad work of the battle-fields it is as well known that there must be large numbers of the wounded. It is to minister to the temporal and spiritual wants of these sick and wounded men that the Christian Commission performs its voluntary offices.

"The character of the Commission was fixed at the meeting of the delegates at the instance of George H. Stuart, Esq., by whose happy forethought and succeeding labors the body was brought into existence. The philanthropic features of the Commission have not been changed. The work as suggested by Mr. Stuart of performing the service of the good Samaritan to the sick of the army and the disabled of the battle-fields is still continued. The area of the work has been greatly extended, and the number of the workmen has been greatly increased. Following, as the Commission has done, in the footsteps of the Army and in the wake of the vessels of the Navy, in the expansion of its labors the obligation has been forced upon it of increasing its laborers and means. Wonderful has been its success in meeting this emergency. An all-wise and overruling Providence has raised up friends as they were needed, and means as they were demanded. Although at the first it was difficult to accomplish the smaller amount of necessary service, it has not been much more so to perform the same over the greatly extended field that is now whitened for the harvest and demands the laborers and the material necessary for the performance of their work. It is not pretended that the service contemplated has been fully performed in the relief of all the suffering and privation that have appeared in the view of the Commission's agents and delegates. Our means have never been adequate to this demand; but as far as the men and the means could be provided they have been appropriated, and although all the needed service could not be rendered, a very great proportion of the suffering necessarily occasioned by the war has been relieved. Had there been more men and more money, the greater had been the service and the more nearly perfect had been its performance.

"As a voluntary association, the Christian Commission has no official relation either to the Government or to the Army and Navy. There is no detriment to the service, however, on this account. The work of the Commission is approved and sanctioned by the Government, and directions have been given that its delegates should be respected and protected, and every possible facility afforded them in the pursuit of their labors. The name of the President of the United States, and the names of a number of the gentlemen of the Cabinet and Generals and other officials of the Army and Navy, have been associated with the Commission, and thereby the connection of the Commission with the Army and Navy service has been rendered as nearly official as is desirable. No surgeon or chaplain of the Army and Navy who understands the relationship of the Commission with the service ever thinks of impeding the progress of the work or of doing anything in its connection that does not facilitate its purpose. But few difficulties have arisen on account of misunderstandings in this relation, and the few that have occurred have been readily adjusted when the proper relationship of the parties were understood.

"An association known as the Baltimore Christian

Association for the relief of the disabled of the camps and hospitals, was in the service before the organization of the Christian Commission. It was fairly at its work in May, 1861, preceding the date of the order establishing the United States Christian Commission. As soon as the Committee of Maryland of the Commission was appointed, the Baltimore Association became auxiliary to the United States Christian Commission, and has ever rendered efficient service in the connection.

"Previous to the date at which the Christian Commission was organized, the Secretary of the Maryland Committee was in treaty with clergymen of Baltimore for the purpose of making application to the Government for the provision of a chaplain service for the hospitals. A correspondence was entered into with persons connected with the hospitals for that purpose. On one occasion, that of a hospital at which four clergymen were in the habit of visiting, an application was made for assistance in obtaining from the Government the appointment of a chaplain for the hospital and one for each of the hospitals then established. The reply to the application was unfavorable. The number of unofficial visitors was said to be, and doubtless were, so great that they were in one another's way. What was wanted was a proper head, and a system by which the work should be regulated. The suggestion was not appreciated that the appointment of a single chaplain with official relations and authority would regulate the attendance of others, and render their assistance of much greater use by being more systematic and regular. Letters were written by the Secretary to members of Congress, but without effect. To President Lincoln is due the honor of having the chaplaincy service established, and from him the Christian Commission has received every necessary evidence of favor, and by his encouraging efforts its service has been rendered much more effective than it could possibly have been without it. By a late act of Congress the rank of the chaplain is that of major, which gives them higher authority and greater influence than they have heretofore had.

"The voluntary service of the United States Christian Commission in the relief of the sick and wounded of the Army and Navy, is rendered almost official by the approval and protection of the Government. It is now making up the deficiencies in the religious service, and in the administration of delicacies to the sick and wounded, that probably could not be otherwise supplied. It is not at all probable that Army and Navy officials, however well remunerated, and however well supplied with means, would answer the demands made upon the Christian Commission. The character of the service indicates the voluntary supply, and in such relation only can the labor be properly performed.

"It is not to be inferred from our remarks in relation to the necessity of the service of the Christian Commission that the Government does not make ample provision for the pursuit of its purpose in the management of the war, nor that the agencies provided are not sufficiently humane for the purpose. Never was there such provision made by any Government for the relief of the sufferings necessarily occasioned in the conduct of a war as there has been by the Government of the United States in the present sad emergency. Surgeons and chaplains have been supplied for regiments and hospitals; and these are sufficient for ordinary purposes. But all the surgeons in the country would be insufficient for the demand upon the service after such battles as have been fought in the present contest. Nor in such emergency could all the religious service that could be secured be sufficient for the supply of the battle-fields and camps and hospitals. It were well therefore that there should be an agency that could wait on the outside and in calmness and with due consideration measure the field demanding the relief, and make provision for its supply.

"Such is the work of the United States Christian Commission. It is waiting in its place outside of the Army, and of any of the official relations of the Government. It has its delegates composed of Christian ministers and laymen of every religious denomination. The supply is always at hand, and with such means as we have, we send them forth wherever their services are needed. The good pleasure of the Lord has hitherto prospered in their hands, and there can be no doubt of the immense service they are now rendering, and may continue to render in the cause of suffering, bleeding humanity.

"The following letter from Secretary Stanton expresses his approval of our Commission and its purpose:

"'WAR DEPARTMENT, WASHINGTON CITY,
April 16, 1864.

"'DEAR SIR: Among the benevolent associations organized by patriotic and charitable men during the present war, none has surpassed, and few, if any, have equaled the Christian Commission in zeal, energy, and disinterested devotion to the humane objects of their institution. Their efficient labors in the field, in the hospital, and in the camp have been felt by soldiers and officers, and have frequently been brought to the notice of this Department. It is not only a pleasure, but I regard it as an official duty to commend the Christian Commission to public confidence and respect, as an institution whose labors cannot fail to contribute greatly to the welfare of our armies.

"'Yours truly, EDWIN M. STANTON,
Secretary of War.'

"The following is an extract from a letter received by the Secretary of the Maryland Committee:

"'No one more heartily sympathizes with the objects, or more highly appreciates the labors of the Christian Commission than your very humble servant, WILLIAM H. SEWARD.'

"Letters of the same nature have been received from President Lincoln and from other members of the Cabinet, as well as from a number of the most distinguished officers of the Army and Navy."

"A friend of the Commission, of active and energetic habits, whose power of thought was rapid and vivid during the process of his absorbing and trying labors, has remembered the events that transpired around him with an interest that has never yet failed to produce an involuntary thrill through his system whenever the recollection of them has occurred. Like the ever-changing visions of a terrific dream the ranks of the fallen have appeared. The living who were badly wounded were seen struggling under bodies of the dead, others crawling over them, apparently for the purpose of reaching places of relief and security, or spots upon which to die. Among the living and the dead were the men of both armies, the enemies that had fought in the sanguinary conflict. The scene was terrific in its ever-varying variety. There were mangled masses of animal matter composed of the bodies and parts of bodies of dead horses, human forms, limbs and heads, with features yet horrible in the contorted lineaments of the death agony; the web-work of iron, wood, leather, and matted clothing, all the shattered implements of war and warlike equipments, and shred-worn habiliments of the soldier. The area of horror thus presented was rendered yet more horrible by the activity everywhere in motion of hundreds of laborers with picks and spades, digging trenches, and dragging into them the bodies of the dead, and covering them with earth. Great was the relief afforded the view in the appearance of the delegates of the Christian Commission with their towels and cloths and pails and basins of water. They were quenching the thirst of the suffering, bathing their foreheads and faces, and washing their wounds, and applying the necessary restoratives to the fainting and exhausted system. They were removing gently, and with the most anxious concern, the bodies of such as would bear it. They were whispering the words of comfort and heavenly consolation to the dying. They were receiving the last messages of love to friends and relatives at home. They were receiving pledges of affection for loved ones and giving assurances of remembrance, and that their dying testimonials and requests should be faithfully and promptly delivered. The same attention and services were rendered the fallen of the enemy that were given to the soldiers of the Union army. Upon the arm of the delegate the head of the dying rebel has reclined; and while assurances of remembrance to friends, were it possible, and words of consolation were spoken, the spirit has passed to its place among the departed.

"On the several occasions when bodies of the enemy, in various numerical force, have invaded the territory held by our troops along the line of the Potomac, in Virginia, Pennsylvania, and Maryland, we have visited in person or sent delegates for service amid the scenes of disaster and bloodshed. On occasions of anticipated invasion, our delegates have been in readiness with stores prepared for the purpose, and they have followed swiftly upon the movements of the armies and performed extended service to the needy they have left upon the fields behind them. In some instances they have barely escaped capture, sometimes with loss. In several instances their clothing and other property have fallen into the hands of the enemy. One of our chaplains, the Rev. Mr. Pormer, on one occasion, escaped with his life, but lost all the clothes and property he had with him; his loss was nearly two hundred dollars.

"Religious services have been established, through the agency of the commission, in many places where they have been needed. At every possible point at which our delegates are laboring, meetings for preaching, experience and prayer have been held. The benefits of this service have been repeatedly acknowledged by government officials and others, who have witnessed their effects not only upon the sick and dying, but upon the soldier in health, and in the active service of the camp. Testimonials of the dying of a most gratifying character are upon the record, and many who are living bear continuous testimony of their effect in the witness of faithfully devoted religious lives.

"A number of terrific battles have been fought during the last year. Through all these the Commission has followed the army, rendering needed service to the dead and wounded of both the contending armies. The cases are but few in which the sufferer of either army has been overlooked; never do we believe has he been willfully neglected. In the wake of these battles we have had experienced delegates. The experience was attained on former occasions of services, and it has rendered the labors of delegates much more ready, as well as much more efficient. Our own experience in arranging for the prosecution of our labors has been valuable to us. It has forced upon us the knowledge of the sort of work we have to perform, and enables us to accomplish it with much greater readiness and ease than were possible when we started in the enterprise. Our field is now much more systematically arranged and much better worked than formerly. Its points of duty generally are distributed with a degree of regularity throughout the departments of the army in the occupancy of our district. The movements of delegates are ordered in such manner as best enables them to communicate with field, local, and traveling agents, with army officials, and with each other. In this order the work of the Commission is rendered comparatively convenient, and is accomplished with a good degree of satisfaction.

"It is a sad reflection that the cost of our continued experience and attainment of proficiency should be the blood of hundreds of thousands of our countrymen, and of thousands of millions of treasure that might be expended in the building up rather than in the destruction of cities, and in the beautifying rather than the devastation of the valuable territory occupied and trodden down by the hostile armies. But our misguided fellow-citizens will have it so. The terrible issue is forced upon us. Painful as is the process, we must educate ourselves for the afflictive service, or leave unaccomplished one of our most important and necessary duties to humanity, to our country, and to our God.

" To the suffering prisoners of the Union army at Richmond we have been able to send relief on various occasions. Our own supplies, without an exception that we have heard of, have reached their destination. The benefits experienced by the starving men, in the receipt of sufficient provisions to relieve their necessities, may well be imagined. Letters have been received from the prisoners acknowledging the receipt of boxes of first quality hams, beef, bread, coffee, tea, sugar, with the best of wines that could be found, etc. These letters have contained expressions of gratitude, and desires for remembrance of friends and families, which are of most touching and interesting character. The like has hardly been recorded in history of such abundance of provisions being sent into the heart of an enemy's home for the relief of the needy captives taken in the pursuit of an imbittered and terrific and dreadfully afflictive war. It is admitted that no such fighting has ever occurred as that which has been recorded of the armies of Anglo-Saxon descent now in the field. It must also be admitted that no such concern has been experienced for the suffering, and no such relief afforded them as that which appears on the records of the Christian Commission. Our history will be a tale of mercy unknown among the archives of the nations of either ancient or modern times. The fallen and afflicted enemy of the battle-field finds a friend and protector in the people against whom his hand has been raised amid the fearful strife of rebellion and war, and the captive in the distant prison of the enemy finds relief and support in the abundance provided and transmitted by the friends from whom he has been separated in his capture.

"Close upon the marches of the army, and fast upon its battle-fields, have been the movements of the Christian Commission. We had scarcely narrated the services of our delegates and ourselves in the battles of the summer of 1863 when the enemy appeared in different places along the line of the Potomac, and not only threatened the States of Maryland and Pennsylvania with invasion, but in several instances actually crossed the river, and appeared on the Maryland and Pennsylvania shores in pursuit of whatever plunder they could find.

"On September 22, 1863, the rebels crossed the Potomac and entered Maryland at Rockville, Montgomery County. They scoured the country for several miles, and secured a considerable amount of plunder in cattle and different kinds of store goods, when they were attacked by the Union troops, and forced to return to their own camping grounds in Virginia. It was not without several skirmishes, in which many lives were sacrificed, and many of both armies disabled, that they were allowed to escape. As early after this raid as September 25, Moseby's men attacked and destroyed a portion of the Orange and Alexandria Railroad. While at their work they were fallen upon by the Union troops and driven back with some slaughter on both sides. Again, October 5, Winchester and Harper's Ferry were attacked and captured by the enemy, who, as usual, held them but a few days, when the federal army drove them out, and retook the captured towns and vicinities. October 7 skirmishes took place near Martinsburgh with various results, in the capture of Union troops by the rebels, and the capture of rebels by the Union troops. On all these occasions men were killed and wounded, and work provided for the delegates of the Christian Commission. Delegates were sent from our office to the scenes of conflict, where their accustomed services were performed with their accustomed success.

"At different periods during the year these raids were repeated. The invasion of July 6 is perhaps the most formidable of the efforts of the kind that transpired in the vicinity during the year. It commenced in the plunder of Frederick City, and was continued in various depredations until after the burning of Chambersburgh, which took place on August 6. The result of these raids left by far the most of the dead and wounded of the enemy on our hands. In hurried retreats it was not possible for them to bury their dead, or to take their wounded from the field. Our hospitals were occupied by large numbers of rebels, on account of whose sufferings the sympathies of our people were excited, and a vast deal of labor and money were expended in their relief. The hospitals at Frederick City were sometimes filled with the wounded of the two armies, while many of the disabled were sent to Baltimore and Washington cities.

"While the raids were in progress along the Upper Potomac, the most severe and sanguinary battles of the campaign were fought during the passage of Gen. Grant's army toward Petersburgh and Richmond. The contest for Fredericksburgh had been severe and bloody, and while the power of possession seemed to be alternately in the Union and rebel forces, a number of very hardly contested skirmishes took place, in which many were killed and wounded on both sides. At length, when the scale was permanently inclined in favor of the Union army, nearly all the wounded of the enemy fell into our hands. The provisions of the hospitals, which were sufficient in all cases for our own wounded, were insufficient for the accommodation of the crippled of both armies. Shelter tents, and such temporary accommodations as could be hastily provided, were brought into use until the men could be conveyed to distant places of security and comfort. On all occasions the delegates of the Commission were near, and ready with their stores for their work of Christian liberality, providing for the sufferer with whatever means they had on hand, laboring with ceaseless and untiring industry until the objects of their greatly excited interest were as comfortable as they could render them.

"Afterward came on the battles of the Wilderness, Chancellorsville, Spottsylvania, North Anna, Coal Harbor, Bermuda Hundred, Weldon, then the siege of Petersburgh and Richmond. The slaughter in these battles was immense. The numbers of the wounded were counted by tens of thousands. They were to be hunted out from among the dead. They were to be taken to the ambulance, or if too badly hurt for the jolting of the ambulance, to the shelter-tent of the field. In these shelter-tents, rapidly constructed to screen the sufferer from the scorching rays of the summer's sun, the surgeons were in waiting with their instruments for amputation and for searching the wounds. In the changes of the armies here from Fredericksburgh to the North Anna, thence to the White House, thence to City Point, there were perils to be encountered unknown in human warfare. At every point the enemy was stationed in force, and it was only through the most extreme perseverance and at the most fearful risk and expense of life and suffering that these necessary objects were accomplished. Sure as the battle and the bloodshed was the appearance of the delegates of the Commission.

"In large numbers from Maryland, and in larger numbers from the central office in Philadelphia, they crowded into our apartments. We were well provided with haversacks and blankets and stores. Haversacks and blankets were delivered to each delegate; the haversack was filled with articles for immediate use, and the boxes were packed and sent by the steamboat, or the railroad, or by the wagon team, as became necessary. In some instances the stores were sent in advance of the delegate, and were in waiting when he arrived. It was indeed cheering, amid the harrowing reflections occasioned by the terrific slaughter of human life, and the fearful mangling of the human form in such multitudes, to witness the eagerness and earnestness with which our men buckled on their armor of peace and humanity, the haversack and the blanket, and hurried out of the office to the depot of conveyance for the field of their labor. It was a sacrifice to them of time and money and strength, and a risk of sickness and accident. But these drawbacks were not in their ▸consideration. The cost was counted in the duty to which they were committed in the relief of their suffering fellow-men. The duty was imperative. It was counted in humanity's covenant with God. It was God's own work in his care over his creatures, and the trust was in God that he would bless his own work and lead his own self-sacrificing servants through it. The hour for the meditation and the formal prayer with them had passed when they appeared for their equipments for the service, and like men engaged in business transactions, or in pursuit of journeys in business relations, they entered their names, and received their supplies and left for the conveyance. We say formal prayer, because Christian men have their hours and their postures for prayer, but they do not always wait for the hours and for the opportunity of placing themselves in the posture. They pray while in the pursuit of their purpose in God's service. They do not always want the books nor even the immediate thoughts of prayer. The very act is prayer; the business is prayer without a word, and apparently without a conscious thought. There is its conscious thought in the act, there is faith in the act, there is trust in the act; the unconscious thought, the faith, the trust, each is prayer, all is prayer. The prayer is in the act. It is the prayer of faith. It is heard on high. It will be answered.

"As we have looked upon these men in the pursuit of their purposes, as anxious as if the large estate were in their view and the extensive business profit to be realized, we have inwardly rejoiced in the view of the better type in which humanity presented itself, and we have prayed that there might be guardian spirits with their unseen protection to shield these messengers of mercy from danger, and conduct them safely through their work. We prayed that there might be such guardian spirits, and we believed there would be. We doubted not that God's invisible leaders and protectors would be with his servants, and that they would be conducted in safety through the period wrested from other necessary life pursuits and devoted to this humane, this Christian-like, this noble service.

"There they were, and there they are, at the front, in the battle's wake waiting for it to subside, and rushing as soon as it is over as if to make amends by Christian services for the sad havoc that selfish humanity would make of itself. In fierce conflict the deed of blood was wrought. In the quiet composure of the peaceful tent the flow of blood was stayed. In maddened frenzy the unfortunate were thrown violently down. In the labor of meekness the fallen was raised up. In the terrific onslaught the bullet and the sword were the agents that brought the ruin. In the merciful intervention the prayer and the word of counsel were the ministers that would have produced the restoration. The intended victim was seized by the hand of Mercy's minister and drawn forth from the place of his peril to be restored to life, to himself, and to the friendships that were as dear as life. The deeds have followed each other in rapid succession. The sword and the bullet have scarcely strewn the soil with their victims when the hand of the delegate has been stretched forth for the relief. The blood was stanched as it flowed from the wound freshly made, and the life of the fallen one has been prevented from passing with the current as it reddened the soil. The living principle still left in the system has been nourished and nursed and encouraged and strengthened, and from the very dust of death the form has been brought forth and restored, and the strong man has once more appeared upon his feet and asked readmission into the ranks of his country's defenders. It is thus that heaven's mercy follows fast in the *personnel* of the Christian Commission in the footsteps of war, and effects the relief of the afflicted, and the restoration amid the ruin.

"It is a strange history that our nationality is now writing. It is the record of the field that tells of the friendly intervention. The tale is written in blood and tears. The mourner stands by the bleeding form, and in the rage and roar and devastation of the battle all is terrible, all is afflicting, all is heart-harrowing, and working wretchedness. But silently, stealthily, and imperceptibly, the relief agent appears. He comes like Mercy's angel with the means of comfort, and with words of consolation. He tells of the trials of earth and of the triumphs of heaven; he points to the brief pilgrimage of sorrow that man passes below, and to the enduring bliss that he is to possess in the world above. The pilgrimage is soon over with its woes and pains and wretchedness, but the bliss is to remain forever. The passing spirit realizes the relation. It looks from its suffering tenement to the joys that await its release. It springs from the clay that holds it in its earthly thrall and flies away to its heavenly rest. So dies the soldier on the field. So passes the human spirit from the wards of the hospital to its home in heaven.

"The history of the hospital must pass along with that of the battle-field. The history of the hospital not only tells of the triumph of the redeemed spirit; it tells also of the restoration of the sufferer, of the reformed life, of the righteousness that superseded the wickedness, of the usefulness that came after the penitence on account of the waste of years, of the earnest labors for God that the willing hands performed when the heart was filled with the love of Christ."

Such is the strange history our nationality is now writing. In this history the Christian Commission must have its part. In the generations of the future its tale of love and mercy must be told. It were well that the hand that binds up the wounds of the sufferer on the battle-field should be painted on the picture that represents the hand with the dagger in its grasp. It were well that the bearer of religious counsels and consolations should be represented on the canvas that exhibits the bearer of the sword. War may devastate and destroy, but the Christian Commission will ever appear in its wake, with the relief and the religious counsel. The field may tell its tale of woe, but the hospital that of the relief.

THE DYING SOLDIER.

"''Tis sweet to die
When Jesus is nigh."

"'Are you the man that sang and prayed last night?' asked a dying soldier just at the break of morning. 'I was one of them,' was the reply. Taking my hand in his he pressed it warmly and said with tearful eyes, 'God bless you, my brother.' 'It was so sweet.' 'It soothed my aching heart so much that the night did not seem half so long as the one before.' A heavenly smile irradiated his countenance and told of inward peace. 'I did not think,' he continued, 'that I should ever hear the voice of prayer and praise again in time.' 'But O! how precious!' 'It brought peace and heaven to my soul.' 'It fell on my crushed and bleeding heart as the dew that descended on the mountains of Zion.'

"We breathed a short prayer for the dying Christian soldier, and left him with ministering angels waiting to convoy his freed spirit to the land of unfading brightness, where garments rolled in blood are never seen, and where there is rest for weary souls. An hour afterward we passed on our rounds the spot thus made with the heavenly light of dying grace. We lingered but a moment to close his eyes and wrap around his manly form the soldier's shroud.

"His countenance, pale and serene, was touchingly beautiful in death.

"The lines of sorrow that shaded his face when we first saw him were no longer visible. They had given place to an expression of peaceful resignation that spoke plainer than words of his triumphant victory over death and sin.

"We gave him a Christian burial, and dropped a tear of sorrow as we remembered the aged mother far away, who for long years had indulged fond hopes for her darling boy, never to be realized.

"God bless the stricken mother was our heartfelt prayer as she reads the letter of Christian sympathy announcing the death, in Christ, of her only son."*

J. R. MILLER, ESQ., field agent for the Christian Commission in the Shenandoah Valley, gives the following interesting particulars:

* Third Report of the Committee of Maryland.

"The battle of Winchester was fought on the 19th of September. It was a most important battle. Previous to the campaign that so auspiciously opened with this engagement, the Valley of the Shenandoah has indeed been our "Valley of Humiliation." There we had suffered defeat after defeat, and the brave men who had fallen on many disastrous battlefields lay scattered over every portion of the valley. But the 19th was a new day in the history of our military operations in that section. For constant and disastrous defeats, we began a series of as brilliant successes as have marked the history of any army of similar power and strength since the war began. Morning saw the enemy proud, defiant, and confident; night found them routed, reduced in numbers by many thousands, flying in disorder, leaving the machinery of war and the debris of battle scattered all along his path. The victory was complete, overwhelming, and destructive; and the news that went to the world filled loyal hearts everywhere with thrills of joy and rejoicing. But victory always costs something, always leaves sad wrecks behind; and amid the shouts of victory on the field, are mingled the groans and wails of the dying; and amid the rejoicings at home over the news of victory, there are always mingled the throbs of broken hearts, for loved ones fall on every field of strife, and every victory sends sadness and desolation to many homes.

"The battle of September 19, while so complete

and successful, was bloody. Hundreds of brave men fell to rise no more, and several thousands fell among the wounded. For several days after the battle the suffering was very great. In addition to our own wounded, there were two thousand of the enemy's wounded left in our hands. Winchester was literally one vast hospital. All the churches and other public buildings were filled, while almost every private house had its quota of wounded and mangled men. There have been but few times since the war began in which there was greater need of external relief. There was nothing left in the country, the Government supplies were all back, the nearest base was Harper's Ferry, over thirty miles distant, and the intervening country was overrun by guerrillas, so that nothing could go forward unless under the protection of a strong military escort. I cannot pass over this period without bearing testimony to the noble and self-sacrificing labors of the loyal ladies of Winchester. When they saw the brave defenders of the old flag, which they still so dearly loved, stricken down in the streets of their city, they at once entered on their work of mercy, and ceased not till all the brave men were made comfortable. They shared their own last morsel with them; they washed and dressed and cheered the weary sufferers, and bent over the dying to catch the last whispered messages to dear ones far away. There are a few names in Winchester which will go down into history garlanded with honors and coupled with deeds of heroism and magnanimity.

"At the time of the battle of the 19th the Christian Commission had no adequate organization in the valley. But immediately after the battle we hired wagons, and pressed forward with supplies and delegates. Then began one of the most important, necessary, and successful works of mercy that it has ever been our lot to perform. Never was sympathy or kind aid more opportune or more welcome. Night and day these men labored among the wounded thousands, washing, dressing, feeding, praying with the dying, burying the dead, and calling upon the living to repent and be saved. And thus the work went on from day to day, constantly increasing in interest and importance. The battles of October followed, and again filled up the hospitals at Winchester with wounded and dying men, and again our hands were full.

"As soon as the railroad was restored, Martinsburg became a place of great importance to our work. Almost every wagon train from the front brought down two, three, or five hundred men on their way to the hospitals of Baltimore and Northern cities. During the first few weeks these men were taken to the churches and other buildings from the wagons, where they remained till the following day. Ride all day in a rough army wagon over a macadamized road, and although strong and healthy you will find yourself at night sore and weary. But have your body mangled and torn, and then go through the same process, and you will think that there is no suffering so intense as yours. In this manner these poor sufferers were brought twenty-two miles or more, with no rest and nothing to eat by the way. We were always apprised of their coming an hour or more before they began to arrive, and large campkettles full of water were placed over the fire, and soon forty or fifty gallons of tea were ready. Then, with tea, crackers, cheese, meats and fruits, our delegates hurried about from place to place till all were fed. Then came the bathing and washing and dressing, and it was usually well nigh morning before all was done; but after a night's hard labor our delegates have always felt amply repaid for their toil in the gratitude of many noble hearts. In the morning the same routine came again, and at noon the brave fellows were placed in the cars for another long, hard ride, and our last act was to make them as comfortable as possible on their hard beds in the cars.

"It does one good to minister to the wants of such sufferers in such a cause, and to see how their hearts overflow with gratitude to their friends who do so much for them. As one of our delegates was bathing the brow of a noble young fellow, and putting on clean garments instead of blood-stained ones, and giving him some delicacies to eat, he raised his tearful eyes, and asked him what prompted him and others of his fellow-laborers to leave their homes and spend their days and nights on the battle-fields and in the hospitals. He answered him: 'We do it because we love Jesus.' Yes, this is the true idea of Christianity: a Christianity that works as well as prays and believes. Jesus, our great pattern, taught us in his life what is the true style of Christian living. He went about doing good, healing the sick, opening the eyes of the blind, unstopping the ears of the deaf, cleansing the lepers, casting out devils. And he says to all of his disciples in all ends of the earth, he says to-night to you and to me: 'Go and do likewise.' 'Freely ye have received, freely give!'

"But this relief work is not our only work. While caring for the temporal wants of our soldiers, and giving them physical comforts, our delegates never forget the thought that these men are beings for immortality, and never fail to bring before their minds, if but in a hastily spoken word as they hurry from cot to cot among thousands, the great truth that they have interests far higher than those of time. Then during the winter campaign, which is always more or less quiet, we enter on our great work of preaching the Gospel. Chapels are erected in every part of our armies, prayer-meetings organized everywhere, and religious newspapers, books, tracts, and Testaments distributed in every regiment. Some of the most interesting prayer-meetings I have ever attended have been held in the army. It seems that there is a warmth and feeling among soldiers in the field and far from their homes that one never sees in the too much stereotyped religious services at home.

"During the winter of 1862 and '63 I was in Falmouth, Va. We organized a prayer-meeting there in an old factory building. The number increased until two or three hundred were present, and the house was filled to overflowing. Evening after evening men rose for prayers, and many expressed a hope of a living interest in the Saviour. Of many remarkable conversions there during those few months I will notice but one. It was so striking and remarkable that I cannot pass it by.

"I was sitting in my office one morning in April, when a strong, athletic man, with bronzed cheeks, entered, and taking a seat, began to converse freely and intelligently. Pretty soon he began to talk of his home, and I could easily see that there was some great load at his heart, and that he had come in to unburden himself. He said he had a wife and two little girls. I asked him if he was a Christian. He said, after a pause and through tears, that he was not. He drew a letter from his pocket, and asked me to read it aloud to him. He said it was from one of his dear little girls. She was but ten years of age, but had wisdom beyond her years. She spoke of her mother and little sister; she told him of her Sabbath-school, and how she loved her teacher and her Bible. Then the tender-hearted child told him how she prayed for her absent father, and then she began to beseech him to become a Christian and to love her Jesus. She spoke of the dangers through which he dayly passed, and implored him to give his heart to God. As I read, the great tears filled his eyes and trickled down his coarse cheeks. He told me he desired to become a Christian. His little girls were praying for him, and his wife and his mother, in Canada, were praying for him, and all were writing to him. And then he had been present at our prayer-meetings, and it seemed, he said, that his way was hedged up; he could not stand all these calls to repentance; brave as he was, this took all his courage away.

"That night at the prayer-meeting he rose and asked the prayers of his fellow-soldiers. Next night he expressed his hope of an interest in the Saviour. From that time he led a consistent life. I believe he was really converted to God, and I believe also that it was by means of the prayers and letters of that little girl that he found rest to his soul. God hears prayers and answers requests.

"At the base of Round Top Mountain, on the bloody field of Gettysburgh, when the angry strife was over, I found his grave. He had fallen for his country, but I trust he is with his Saviour.

"Among the first to fall on that bloody Sabbath,

at Fredericksburgh, the 3d of May, was a young man from Newburyport, Massachusetts. He had been constant in his attendance on our prayer-meetings, and faithful in his living, and had already given evidence that he was a true soldier of the cross. I found him soon after he had fallen; a ball had passed through his temples, destroying both eyes. When I spoke to him he knew me by my voice, grasped me by the hand and said, 'I am mortally wounded and soon must die.' I said, 'Charlie, do you feel willing to die here?' 'O yes,' said he, 'I have done the last for my God and my country. I have a dear mother at home whom I would like to see once more, and I would like to die at home with them; but I must die here, and God's will be done.' 'Is Christ as precious to you now, Charlie, as he used to be in the prayer-meetings?' 'O yes,' he said, 'far more precious. Write to my friends, and tell them that although my eyes are gone, this last hour is the brightest hour of my life.' Thus died this most noble young man. Far from home, and far from the dear ones that make home happiest and best, he died triumphantly. Jesus was near, and that was enough to lighten the darkness, to smooth the pillow, to ease the pain, and to bear the soul high above the fears and anxieties of this world.

"A young officer was found on one of our battle-fields mortally wounded. He had his Bible in his hand as he lay calmly awaiting the moment of death.

His Bible was opened at the eighth chapter of Romans, and with his pencil he had traced around the first and last five verses of that chapter. Those verses have ever since possessed a value and sweetness to my mind that but few verses in the Bible possess. Think of a dying man pausing on the brink of life, while eternity's vast depths opened up before him, to trace his pencil around that glorious truth, 'There is therefore now no condemnation to them who are in Christ Jesus;' and that other declaration, that nothing in heaven or earth, nor among the powers of the air, can separate him from the love of Christ. It was worth living a whole lifetime in toil, privation, and danger to witness such a death. When asked if he had any message to send to his mother, he answered, 'Send her my Bible and sword, and tell her that I died in the arms of my Saviour.' Worlds could not buy that Bible from his mother. It is far too precious. Those pencil tracings made by that faint hand, just as death was completing its work, and around such precious words, are worth more than lines of gold, because they tell the story of that young man's life and death for Christ."

Rev. L. Hartsough, of the Methodist Episcopal Church, and agent of the Commission at Point Lookout, made the following remarks:

He stated that his heart had been stirred by the thrilling thoughts expressed by Brother Miller, and could appreciate them the better on account of the experience that he had had in the same work. Among the many precious things that were coming to the knowledge of the Christian Commission delegates, that cheered their hearts and encouraged them in their work, was the following beautiful waif that will speak for itself, and which the speaker read amid the tears of the audience:

"A young man in one of our southern hospitals,* wounded in the first fight at Vicksburg, when asked by a Christian gentleman (Bro. Burnell) if he had a Testament, said, 'Yes, but my eyes are growing dim, and I can't see to read such fine print now.' The gentleman gave him his, which was larger type, in exchange. In the young soldier's Testament were written these words:

"LAWSON WOOD.
"FROM YOUR MOTHER.
" My son, fear God."

And then followed, in a different handwriting, these words:

"'On the field of battle, mother,
All the night alone I lay,
Angels watching o'er me, mother,
Till the breaking of the day;
I lay thinking of you, mother,
And the loving ones at home,
Till to our dear cottage, mother,
Boy again, I seemed to come.

"'He to whom you taught me, mother,
On my infant knee to pray,
Kept my heart from fainting, mother,
When the vision passed away;

* Nashville.

In the gray of morning, mother,
  Comrades bore me to the town,
From my bosom, tender fingers
  Washed the blood that trickled down.

"'I must soon be going, mother,
  Going to the home of rest;
Kiss me as of old, mother,
  Press me nearer to your breast.
Would I could repay you, mother,
  For your faithful love and care;
God uphold and bless you, mother,
  In the bitter woe you bear.

"'Kiss for me my little brother,
  Kiss my sister, loved so well;
When you sit together, mother,
  Tell them how their brother fell;
Tell to them the story, mother,
  When I sleep beneath the sod,
That I died to save my country,
  All from love to her and God.

"'Leaning on the merits, mother,
  Of the One who died for all,
Peace is in my bosom, mother;
  Hark, I hear the angels call!
Don't you hear them singing, mother?
  Listen to the music's swell.
Now I leave you, loving mother;
  God be with you; *fare you well*.'

"Two days after, this gentleman called to see Lawson Wood, but he had gone home to Jesus."*

The work commenced by the Commissions, and which has been so eminently successful, will be continued and expanded by other agencies, until our bleeding country shall be healed of its wounds, and its unity be restored and permanently established.

The government will adopt measures for the resto-

---

* Thanksgiving service, held by the U. S. Christian Commission, on the evening of November 24, 1864, in Light-street Methodist Episcopal Church, Baltimore.

ration of the disaffected states to their former position and privileges, to their ancient love for the Union, and sympathy with a sound national policy. The disruption of those states left the body politic ghastly and gory; the measures of the government in due time will be to bind up, to mollify, and to cure the wounds. The present work is that of the skillful surgeon, who, in certain conditions of a wound, finds it necessary to use the probe and the scalpel; the future will be more especially that of healing and administering cordials. The people who have blindly rushed into secession and rebellion will see their error and return to their allegiance, and they will be welcomed to the common brotherhood of states, and reinstated in all their legitimate rights and privileges. Old feuds and heartburnings will be forgotten, sectional animosities will cease, and a common platform of human rights and equal justice will tend to annihilate antagonisms, and to mould the whole American people into one homogeneous mass. The violence which has occasioned the temporary estrangement of the southern states will yield to the stern discipline of war, and be succeeded by the feelings of confraternity and brotherly affection. The unity of the states will then be a common faith, and the object and end of a united, continued, and uninterrupted endeavor. As we have "one Lord, one faith, and one baptism," so we shall have one political creed and shall be one people.

The several states will co-operate in the great and good work of restoration. Commerce between them will be revived. The old channels of intercourse and trade will be opened and occupied. The rivers, harbors, and railways will be crowded, and interchange of commodities between the North and South will settle the conviction of mutual dependence and promote the prosperity and wealth of both sections. The eastern, the middle, the western, and the southern states will regard themselves, not as so many independencies, but as parts of one grand nationality. The rights of the several states will be considered as the rights of sisters of the same family, and not as the rights of independent governments. All the stars of the national galaxy shall shine with their own peculiar luster; and although one star may differ from another in glory, there will be no conflicts between them. The laws of commerce will be so many bonds of union; mutual dependence will beget mutual respect, and the advantages arising from the exchange of commodities will encourage forbearance and friendship. The union of the states will promote the happiness and prosperity of each, and the prosperity of each will redound to the honor and glory of the whole. Then shall be realized the spirit and intent of the prophecy, "The envy also of Ephraim shall depart, and the adversaries of Judah shall be cut off: Ephraim shall not envy Judah, and Judah shall not vex Ephraim."

ITS TRIAL AND ITS TRIUMPH. 297

> O Peace! thou source and soul of social life:
> Beneath whose calm, inspiring influence
> Science his views enlarges, art refines,
> And swelling commerce opens all her ports;
> Blest be the man divine who gives us thee!
>
> THOMSON.

The people by every possible means must encourage friendly intercourse and mutual confidence. All distance and exclusiveness, envy and sectional jealousies, should be avoided, and a community of interests should be a feeling more than a mere sentimentality. Let the people of the North and of the South mingle together freely: let travel, business relations, and matrimonial alliances be encouraged. Let those refugees from the South who find it agreeable, and can make it profitable to settle themselves in business in the North, do so; and our soldier boys, whose tastes and interests lead them in that direction, find for themselves homes in the sunny South. A reciprocity of kindly feelings and a thorough acquaintance will finally overcome sectional prejudices.

> Friendship is no plant of hasty growth;
> Though planted in esteem's deep-fixèd soil,
> The gradual culture of kind intercourse,
> Must bring it to perfection.
>
> JOANNA BAILLIE.

It has often been said since the war of the rebellion commenced that the South and the North can never live together again under the same government; that the friction of the war has so destroyed all respect and confidence between the two classes that they can never be restored. This is an ignorant and prejudiced view of the subject. Time is a great healer of the wounds of the soul and under proper circumstances, will finally efface the deepest scars. History furnishes an abundance of evidence that two peoples may be reconciled and live in harmony after the most terrible wars between them. The tribe of Benjamin, after being nearly extinguished by a sudden outbreak of war with the other tribes, occasioned by the murder of a Levite's concubine at Gibeah, in the days of the Judges, became reconciled by sympathy and measures of conciliation, and ever after lived in the most amicable relations with the tribe of Judah. England and Scotland for centuries were engaged in the most cruel wars, and seemed to be influenced by the most invincible antipathies, and yet they finally became united under the same government. The leaders in a quarrel, when it is over, lose their power for mischief, and the masses, who are their victims, settle down into quiet submission to the natural order of things. It will be but a short time before the fomenters of the great southern feud will be out of sight and out of mind. The whole generation of them will pass away like the dew before the rising sun. The people are not always to be mystified. The reign of passion is short. After a brief interruption by violence, reason and common sense, conscience and religion, will finally resume their sway. The better feelings of the human heart once in the ascendant, mob violence and brute force give place to law and order, and peace returns to bless the world.

> Lend once again that holy song a tongue
> Which the glad angels of the advent sung,
> Their cradle anthem for the Saviour's birth,
> "Glory to God, and peace unto the earth!"
> Through the mad discord send that calming word
> Which wind and wave on wild Gennesareth heard;
> Lift in Christ's name his cross against the sword!
>
> WHITTIER.

The last but not the least restorative which I notice, and which the whole country should pray for, is a general outpouring of the Holy Spirit. The chastened feelings with which the sufferings and horrors of the war will be regarded, it may be hoped, will be favorable to religious reflection, humiliation, and prayer. The Church should come out of the struggle nerved with fresh power, and inspired with an aggressive spirit. During the war she has lifted high the standard of the cross, and has contended nobly against abounding iniquity. She has interposed her intercessions between an overwhelming storm of divine vengeance and the country; she has sent her sons into the army to fight, and her daughters have remained at home to pray. Her sympathies and her prayers have reached to heaven. God has witnessed her struggles, heard her prayers, and sent down his blessings upon the government, the army and navy, and the whole people. She has passed through experiences which will have prepared her for a new and vigorous campaign "when this cruel war is over." A great revival of religion will be the pressing want of the country, and the natural subject of thought and object of labor with every devout heart. The earnest, active piety of the whole Church will move, yea, is moving now straight toward this mark. Already the cloud of mercy is rising in the heavens the bigness of a man's hand, betokening an abundant shower. A mighty rain of righteousness will heal broken hearts, sanctify poverty, cheer desolate hearths, and harmonize the discordant elements of society. The grace of God, rich, full, and free, is the great resource of the nation in these times of peril, and will be in all future emergencies, and will be vouchsafed in answer to fervent and believing prayer.

THE END.

www.ingramcontent.com/pod-product-compliance
Lightning Source LLC
Chambersburg PA
CBHW032043230426
43672CB00009B/1452